# NUK TESSLI

*The Life of a Wilderness Dweller*

## CHRIS CZAJKOWSKI

ORCA BOOK PUBLISHERS

Canadian Cataloguing in Publication Data
    Czajkowski, Chris.
    Nuk Tessli

    ISBN 1-55143-133-5

1. Czajkowski, Chris. 2. Frontier and pioneer life — British Columbia. 3. Wilderness areas — British Columbia. 4. Coast Mountains (B.C. and Alaska) — Biography. 5. Women — British Columbia — Biography. I. Title.
FC3845.C56Z49 1999   971.1'104'092   C99-910039-4   F1089.C7C92 1999

Library of Congress Catalog Card Number: 98-83017

Canadä
Orca Book Publishers gratefully acknowledges the support of our publishing programs provided by the following agencies: the Department of Canadian Heritage, The Canada Council for the Arts, and the British Columbia Arts Council.

Cover design by Christine Toller
Cover photograph and interior illustrations by Chris Czajkowski
Printed and bound in Canada

Orca Book Publishers
PO Box 5626, Station B
Victoria, BC  Canada
V8R 6S4

Orca Book Publishers
PO Box 468
Custer, WA   USA
98240-0468

01 00 99   5  4  3  2  1

*To Joyce Dorey*

Much of this material was originally written in the form of letters to family and friends—Joyce Dorey, to whom this book is dedicated, was one of these recipients. A few were composed for Peter Gzowski's "Morningside" on CBC Radio. Parts of other chapters appeared, in a different form, in nature magazines such as: *Wildflower, Cordillera, Marshnotes* and *Wingspan*.

# acknowledgements

Bob and Patrick Cohen, and Francie Wilmeth, trappers and outfitters, were particularly helpful in the beginning when I made the first saw cut on virgin land. Gloria and Roger Folsom accommodated me during my early trips to the post office until their attic became embarrassingly full of stored possessions and it became necessary to seek a whole cabin at the Nimpo Lake Resort as an outside base. The postmistresses at Nimpo are to be thanked, first Cathy Simon, and later Mary Kirner, for processing large bags of outgoing mail, each package accompanied by an array of complicated instructions. Mary also owns the Nimpo Lake Resort. Lora Vaughn (at the time the book was written) ran Avnorth, the floatplane company I generally employ, and she was always trotting over to the store or manipulating mail and freight on my behalf. Her husband, Floyd, a pilot of many years' experience, has put up with my eccentric loads of freight, my perennial lack of funds, and my almost manic reluctance to fly. Most of these duties now fall largely under the auspices of Donna and Ben Davidson, and Lois Bowman.

Several residents of Nimpo Lake have their own planes and they periodically drop in for coffee, bringing mail and whatever fresh goodies are available at the store. Nick Christiansen, Frank Cherne, Terry Brant and Lois Bowman operate a number of private radio repeaters and have given me permission to use their frequencies. Frank Cherne is the genius behind the setting up of my radiophone and figuring out how to prevent my dog from chewing the aerial. Nick Christiansen flies Mary Kirner in for visits and explains technical information about radiophones and solar power in a language I can understand. And finally, special thanks to Mary once again: an unreserved friend of unlimited generosity to everyone with whom she has ever had contact.

# table of contents

# prologue

*... to reside*
*In thrilling region of thick-ribbed ice*
*To be imprisoned in the viewless winds*
*And blown with restless violence round about the pendant world*

William Shakespeare, *Measure for Measure*

January 22, 1992. A soft, mild, pre-dawn darkness lit dimly by the indirect phosphorescence of the surrounding blanket of snow. There is no wind and the night is without sound: no bird, no night creature, no traffic, no neighbour. The nearest human beings are twenty miles to the east and even they are isolated and scattered; their shelters womblike islands of warmth in the night-bound winter forest. At this moment they are likely sleeping, their generators stilled, their banked fires ticking low. My own light source is probably the only visible manifestation of human occupation for some considerable distance. It, however, needs no cacophonic motor to feed it. A single flame, it pushes against the darkness feebly, a pinprick of energy, a counterfeit star, the farthest point in a far-flung constellation of humanity.

I have no clock and there are no stars or moon to show me the time, but I know that it is morning. While breakfast cooks I reach for the radio. It picks up a signal perhaps one day in three, and then only in the dark hours. I never hear the news in summer and, in winter, when the aurora is flying or when there is snow falling somewhere over the three hundred miles of unpeopled mountains between my cabin and Vancouver, it cannot reach me. The mildness of the thickened darkness that shrouds the window could well mean snow, so I do not expect much. Not that I care greatly. The utterances of The Voice Of The Moment have little bearing on reality. It is winter, which means the lake is frozen and I must chop ice or melt snow for water. Also I need to keep my chimney clean and my roof sound and the woodbox full.

In that outer world that hums so urgently over the wires, wars and disasters come and go. The names might change—and sometimes not even those—but the tones and platitudes of The Voice never vary. Of course, the victims are to be pitied, but there is far more horror that never comes to our notice in this way. Each civilization creates its own dogma of importance, its own values, its own greeds, and its own fashionable veneers. The voices I hear are qualified by the subliminal conditioning of a city of a million souls in the mild, coastal climate of Western Canada. It is as simple—and as specific—as that. The announcers might shape their mouths around earth-shattering events but how little their platitudes encompass life beyond their walls.

But our planet is a small place and in my chosen corner of it I am curious about those of its human endeavours and triumphs that the media deem noteworthy enough to pass on. Without TV, newspapers, telephone or regular mail, the radio is my only contact with that world. And while the wars and disasters make little immediate impact on whether the water bucket or woodshed is full, they will in the long run, for there is no movement, no decision, no destruction in this world that does not eventually have some kind of environmental impact. I might prefer to live apart from those crowded, artificial satellites by whose standards most people measure existence, but I could not isolate myself from them even if I wanted to. Twenty miles from the nearest road and neighbour I can filter much of the detritus of modern civilization and absorb what I need, but I am still undeniably part of the confusion and wonder of this sphere that we call Earth.

And so, in the dark hours of the morning of January 22, 1992, I turn on the radio. A voice is just audible through the static, but it is not one I recognize; sometimes CBC Vancouver is squeezed out by Washington or California stations; sometimes, by a quirk of atmospherics, Calgary comes through. I strain to hear—and am amazed. I am not listening to a Canadian signal at all, nor even one from anywhere along the Pacific coast. The broadcast is coming live and direct, all the way from Cape Canaveral, Florida. Roberta Bondar, Canada's first woman astronaut, is about to be launched into space.

The idea of being able to listen to a live event two thousand miles away is almost as exciting as the launch itself—more so perhaps because the launch can only be imagined, whereas the reporter is immediate and real. Thus must the first wireless listeners have crouched around their crackling sets earlier in this century. How quickly subsequent generations have become immune to such wonders; how easily they have accepted that giant step to the moon; how over-exposed they are to so many similar miracles that their only roads to excitement are the media's synthesized violence and the lure of recreational drugs.

As the voice swells and fades across the airwaves, nothing much seems to be happening down on Cape Canaveral. There is a lot of calm counting and technical jargon. It becomes apparent that the launch is to be delayed. I visualise Ms. Bondar cocooned in her module and wonder what is going through her mind.

And I get to thinking. We are not so different, Ms. Bondar and I. It is not just our sex, age and accomplishments that have parallels— she is two years older than myself and we are both women who have gone beyond the parameters of convention—it is also our immediate situations which can be compared.

There she is in her technological womb, physically cut off from all humanity, and yet totally unable to survive without it. Soon she will hang apart from the earth, remote, isolated, and yet undeniably attached to it. Her umbilical cord might be invisible, but no foetus could be more thoroughly nourished. Her well-being depends upon a huge amount of accumulated knowledge combined with enormous attention to detail. Without this vast history of research, her survival would be no more than a gleam in imagination's eye.

And I, in a rough log shelter cobbled together with my own two hands, in the silence of the dark winter forest, am not so very differently placed. Without doubt, I have more options for independent action should something go wrong. If the atmospherics are sympathetic I can radio for a plane and in forty minutes be by the road, or be at a hospital in a couple of hours. If I wish for company, I can don snowshoes, load camping gear onto my packdogs and be at the neighbours' within two or three days. If my woodpile is lean I can go out and fell another tree; if my shelter breaks I have the skills and materials to fix it. If my food is low I have a fair chance of acquiring something to eat—although wild food is scarce at this altitude—and in an extreme emergency I could always eat the dogs. And clean air and clean water are so endlessly abundant that they never even have to be considered.

But I, too, am a child of the modern age and basic survival is not all I want from life. I would not choose to contemplate this isolation without the backup from innumerable sources in the outside world. It is a common conceit to think of a wilderness dweller as being totally self-contained and divorced from the rest of society, but even the most isolated people have some kind of connection with others of their species and I am far from being a hermit. I have chosen a romantic place to live, but one whose climate precludes growing little more than radishes; even the indigenous peoples rarely came here, for wild food was much more easily obtained elsewhere. Thus the bulk of my provisions must be brought from outside. I had logs for building, and I cut some of them into boards, but a lot of my construction supplies and tools were also fetched from the outside world. My cabin is stuffed with books, art materials and the bric-a-brac of an existence that extends far beyond these four walls. I must pay taxes and rents to the government, and fill in endlessly changing bureaucratic forms about my tenure to the land. I rely on floatplanes to transport all supplies, as well as any visitors and occasionally myself.

Like Roberta Bondar, I am secure in my chosen isolation, apart from the world and able to look upon it with detachment, and yet supported by it and inextricably bound to it.

*Chris Czajkowski*

Across the lake, the darkness is separating into shades and the land is beginning to detach itself from the sky. I am an early riser and I love the dawn; I built this cabin so that I could watch it emerge every day that I am here.

There is not a lot to see in this deep-blue winter twilight. The closer trees which frame the shore are blotched with snow; the blanketed expanse of the lake is pale and unmarked; the islands of wind-bent trees hunch like dark ships in the night.

With daylight comes the lifting of the ionosphere and the subsequent fadeout of the signal from Florida. It is perfect weather there, apparently, clear with a small wind, and if there had been no delays, Ms. Bondar would have been beyond the stratosphere by now. I had looked forward to listening at that momentous instant of lift-off, but because of the limitations of my chosen world, it is not to be. Will the shuttle take off as planned, or will the launch be aborted? I will have to try the radio again tomorrow to see if I can pick up any news.

Of what is Ms. Bondar thinking, strapped to her seat, as she lies, awaiting her fate? Many people will be wishing you well at this moment, Roberta, and from my tiny, earthbound corner of the planet I salute you also. You are about to achieve something towards which you have been cultivating your ambitions for a very long time. Our aspirations might be different, but I like to think our orbits have much in common. I understand exactly why you are there.

# chapter 1

# bear facts #1

*Bears and humans have never gotten along very well ...*

Ben Gadd, *Handbook of the Canadian Rockies*

The first time the bear broke into my cabin was in the spring of 1991. I had been outside since the beginning of April, tree-planting in the East Kootenays, that section of British Columbia that separates Alberta from Montana. Spectacular scenery there, too, if you could ignore the hideous clearcuts which overran much of the terrain. But the Rockies are a very different range to my own granite Coast Mountains with their steep, forested plunges to the sea.

When I left my truck at the end of the logging road, prior to hiking back to my cabin, it was already the second half of June. At Nimpo Lake, twenty-six air miles north, the ice had gone out six weeks before; it had likely left my place three or four weeks later. There would be a lot of snow still in the alpine areas and the creeks and rivers would be raging.

Usually I am alone for this first spring hike over the mountains, but this time another hiker was tagging along. An avid canoeist, he had done very little backpacking but was amply fit enough to revel in the sweeping views and bursts of early flowers that coloured the two long days of our trip. It was an exhilarating time: rich, blue spring sky; blinding white snow; the newly naked tundra a roar of snowmelt. As we descended through the upper reaches of the forest to my lake the west wind flexed his muscles and tossed spurts of foam over the long ultramarine swells of the water. It would not have been wise to cross directly to the cabins in these conditions, so we opted for the long way round, down to the foot of the lake behind Crescent Island where the water would be calm and we could avoid going broadside to the waves. Along the main body of the lake, the big swells pushed us from behind, slewing the stern of the little boat with each thrust. White horses pawed the swells alongside and the water sang and hissed with the wind. The lagoon behind the island was smooth enough to have only a riffle marring the surface, but at its end we had to swing back into the wind and paddle like souls demented, knees braced wide, until we slid into the last few yards of shelter beside the wharf.

And thus the first look at the cabin since April. The roof was still on and the chimney still snug in the wire bracing I had rigged up after the snow had swept it to the ground one year. Everything seemed orderly and in place.

The door is enclosed by a porch around the end furthest from the wharf, where it is most sheltered from the west wind and the drifting winter snow. The first intimation that something might be amiss was not evident until we rounded the corner. Skis and poles were tossed about the porch and several boxes of odds and ends like string and cans (which *might* be useful one day) had been raked from their shelves. Nothing, however, seemed seriously out of place—there is always a mess of some sort to deal with when I come home in the spring—and it could well have been the work of squirrels who lose no time in appropriating the place when I am gone. But squirrels could not have made the deep, V-shaped groove next to the home-made wooden bolt that fastened the door. The bolt was still wired in place; I slid it across and swung the door open.

Two of the cabin's windows face west. They are out of sight from any of the angles a human might use to approach the cabin, but that was the way the bear had come in. Both shutters were off, the screens were ripped and one of the windows had disintegrated into a pow-dering of glass dust and slivers. Bedding, books, kitchenware and

*Chris Czajkowski*

furnishings were tossed and tangled like a garbage dump. My feet crunched on cutlery, splintered wood and broken glass. Wind swirled papers, pine needles and shriveled alder leaves.

I'd had first-hand experience of a couple of other bear break-ins during the thirteen years I have lived in the wilderness and had been dutifully impressed with not only the destructive power of these animals but also their purposefulness in making an entry. Once they get the idea they want to be inside, there is very little that will stop them. So I had resigned myself to this probability and had tried to design my cabins accordingly. I'd heard of such strategies as making door and window mats of beds of nails; but my cabins had a lot more windows than the average wilderness shelter and the ground beneath them was very rocky and uneven and would have required a complicated structure to hold the boards. They would also have looked very ugly. Shutters were another suggestion, and in fact the west windows had possessed them; not, however, against the vagaries of animals but to protect the glass from snow that piles up on that side. The shutters worked well enough for their purpose but their attachment was flimsy and it was this that Mr. Bear had casually swiped away. I could have tried spiking their seating and the surrounds of the windows with a barrage of outward-pointing nails, but to make that kind of structure strong enough, it would have to be permanent, and I simply did not want to live in a place bristling with hardware like a porcupine with a Rambo fixation.

The attic, therefore, had been designed to store food and breakables—not that I could hope to build the top of the cabin any more solidly than the bottom but, I reasoned, to break in upstairs, a bear would have to climb the walls and hang on with at least three limbs so would have a lot less agility and power at his disposal. The downstairs door had been lightly constructed in the hopes that it would present the easiest target for a break-in, for that would be the simplest to repair. The windows were the next simplest (they would not be difficult to mend although the replacement of glass posed logistical problems); the walls and roof would be the hardest to fix.

But I had not been smart enough. I had made the mistake of leaving flour on the ground floor. Experience had shown me bears were drawn primarily to strongly aromatic items: rotting fish, meat both fresh and old, garbage, even gas. But flour?

Behind the stove had been two stone crocks and a white plastic bucket with a close-fitting lid, the kind you acquire if you have friends in the restaurant business. Whole-wheat flour had been packed into the larger crock; white in the smaller one and rye flour in the bucket. I had deemed them too heavy to lug upstairs, and in any case had presumed them to be safe.

The bear, however, had been delighted. Every container had been licked squeaky clean. The five-gallon crock still stood behind the stove where I had left it, but the smaller one, its opening presumably too small for the bear to get his nose into, had been packed out through the broken window and dropped on a rock. Both halves were as sparklingly immaculate as a wine glass in a dishwasher advertisement. The lid of the bucket had been pried loose but oddly enough without the tiniest scratch, even though I always had found it a real chore to get off. And this despite the fact that most of the pots and metal containers under the kitchen bench had been gouged and pierced; some of the lighter vessels were as crushed as discarded chocolate wrappers. Bears are renowned for their strength and powers of destruction, but I have noticed before how they also have a great deal of delicacy and finesse when they wish.

The floorboards covering the root cellar had been tossed aside, as had the layer of sheep fleeces laid over the contents to protect them from freezing. (It had still been full winter when I had left.) Interestingly, although the bear had stirred the potatoes, carrots, jars and cans into a jumbled heap, he had not attempted to take a bite out of anything, which was very fortunate: if he had broached a can of fruit, everything would have been ravaged. Among the mess there was, however, another manifestation of the bear's dexterity.

It is not a very convenient root cellar, being simply a hole under the floor. It protects the food from the cold well enough, but access is only from the top and to haul anything out I must lie on my stomach and reach down. I was pawing about among the root vegetables and cans and fleece in an effort to survey the damage when my hand touched a clammy, flaccid, finger-length object which, when unearthed, appeared to be covered in a matted grey pelt. *Dead mouse!* said my brain and I dropped it at once. There were more of them, peeping among the debris. They were not mice at all—they were dill pickles gone mouldy. Somehow the bear had unscrewed the lid of the jar and the pickles had been released to make their contribution to the root cellar's ecology.

A few ornaments were broken and books chewed (in particular a large thesaurus which had impressive tooth holes an inch deep near its spine), but thankfully the stove and chimney were intact, so I did not have soot to add to the disaster as had once happened in another cabin I'd been tenanting. The attic was inviolate, so most of my food was untouched; the only real damage had been to the window.

The bear had obviously not been quite sure what to make of this strange, insubstantial barrier. If he was the same animal who had repeatedly broken into the trap cabins in the area, glass was something he would not have experienced as their small openings had been covered with plastic film when in use and metal from flattened tin cans or heavy slabs of wood bristling with spikes when the trapping season had ended. (Not that this had stopped Mr. Bear: he had torn the metal coverings like paper and split and splintered thick limbs like matchwood had even, on one occasion, ripped apart a wall in his efforts to get inside. And for what? A crunch or two at a coffee can whose contents he didn't like—the brown grains had simply spilled through the holes—and an unproductive lick at a frypan which might have had the remnants of a smell. Bears, it would appear, develop their own brand of cabin fever.)

All my windows were old and multi-paned but it was not the feeble dividers which had presented the bear with his challenge. It was the glass which had given him pause. Having watched bears at work, I could imagine him examining the peculiar, cold, hard, invisible barrier, his head swaying back and forth, trying to figure the best way to deal with it. In the end, judging by the spray of glass fragments, the animal must have launched himself through the window with considerable force: shards were showered clear across the room.

Then he had apparently turned his attention to the food but, appetite satisfied, it was the glass that once more gained his attention. Every single window pane—and there were thirty-eight of them still intact—every single pane had been investigated with a slobbery, floury nose. Every piece of glass was smeared, from corner to corner, with an encrusted film of dried, floury glue.

Well! I would have had to clean the cabin after a three-month absence anyway, and the broken window was a nuisance as it would be some weeks before I would be able to organise new glazing, but otherwise there was not a lot of harm done. The two west windows were the same size and as I liked to look out of the broken one while I sat on the seat, I switched the good one into its space and put builder's plastic over the other. In inclement weather the shutter would have to go back on as well; it would make the back of the cabin a little dark, but at this time of year the days were long and I was not planning on spending a lot of time inside anyway.

The guest cabin was untouched, presumably because no food had been stored there. My client made himself at home while I cleaned

*Chris Czajkowski*

up and did not seem worried put out by the bear's record of achievements. He lived in a rural area in the Kootenays and seemed familiar with nature and much of her machinations so I gave his indifference little thought. My guiding assignment had finished with our arrival and the client was now going to rent the guest cabin and amuse himself for a while. He was a solitary man who enjoyed his own company, so I asked him how he would feel if I left him alone for a couple of days while I built a bridge along the trail towards the road. It was a job I wanted to do as soon as possible to take advantage of the high water I would need to float the logs to the site. Also, as I expected to spend a lot of time in the water, the hot sunny weather we were having was ideal. The rapturous gleam in the client's eyes was answer enough and, as I also love to be alone—everything seems more intense and tangible then—I had no problem understanding his enthusiasm at seeing the back of me.

I use a variety of routes to travel to Nimpo Lake but, no matter which way I go, I have to cross at least one river on the way. So far, my preferred summer route involved wading a tributary which was shallow but about a hundred yards wide; even so, during spring run-off the central channel was too deep and slippery to be negotiated safely, especially when carrying a pack. The previous fall I had explored upstream about half a mile from the ford and found a series of islands and stepping stones which spanned almost the whole width of the river with the exception of a single, deep, narrow channel. Prominent rocks that flanked this channel looked as though they might be suitable to hold two foot-logs clear of the water.

With the help of the dogs, I backpacked a small chainsaw, gas, axe, come-along, ropes, a roll of heavy-gauge wire, pliers, a few large spikes, and food and camping gear for a couple of days. The river crossing was about two hours' hike away from home and about five hundred feet higher, which meant the forest was even sparser and scrubbier than that around the cabin: it took some time to find trees tall enough to span the gap.

I had moved all the logs for the two cabins with a come-along, so I knew that it could be done, but it was incredibly labour-intensive to fall and trim two trees, winch them inch by inch to the water, then prod and float them across a wide, shallow part of the river to the

narrow channel. At the last, the current was a help, but it was also a hindrance as I could no longer stand in the water and the force kept trying to slide the logs where I did not want them to go. With only one winch and one set of ropes (I could not have carried any more) I had to yank at one end of the log, disengage the apparatus and haul it across the river (in a circuitous wade that took me well beyond the reach of the current), link everything up again and pull at the other end, sometimes only an inch or two, before I had to take everything apart again and haul the equipment back. For most of the two days I was up to my waist in water, but the weather was glorious, and the task, although frustratingly slow, was a challenge for my meagre engineering skills. Once the grunt work was over I quite enjoyed it: I was also very much relishing my first dose of solitude in nearly three months.

It was late morning on the third day when I arrived back home. As my canoe slid into the quiet stretch of water by the wharf I was a little disconcerted to find the boat that the client had used had been pulled up so sloppily onto the wharf it was teetering on its keel. It was neither overturned nor tied and a gust of wind might easily have toppled it into the water. I would not have expected a man with my client's canoeing experience to leave it that way.

I made both boats secure, tramped along the wooden walkway to the back porch of my cabin, and opened the door.

The bear had been back.

*Chris Czajkowski*

He had used the same hole to gain entry, and as I had so thoughtfully switched windows for him, I now had a second pile of broken glass. This time, however, there seemed to have been no hesitation on the bear's part as to how he should deal with it; an upraised paw swept downward, and all six panes and the divisions that separated them had been reduced to neat heaps of slivers and chunks of putty on both sides of the sill.

The somewhat rickety table I had cobbled together and which had survived the first intrusion lay pretty much in its component parts. There had been no food at all downstairs—but the bear had discovered solar power. Two six-volt batteries for a small photovoltaic system had been flown in the previous winter. They were stored under a bench. The bear had dumped one of them and a brown stain ran across the wide, home-made floorboards and under my bed. A hand-stitched rug my mother had made was bleached and holed in the middle and a couple of brown blotches, distinctly bearpaw-shaped, lay on the floor beside it.

The acid had soaked into some cardboard boxes that had been stuffed under the bed. The bear apparently liked his snacks spiked, for he had packed one of the cartons out of the window and eaten it—very carefully—leaving the contents, mostly unresolved manuscripts, in an undisturbed pile among the rocks. Fortunately, there had been no rain and little wind, or all the papers would have been lost. There seemed to be little other real damage, but the mess, as before, was appalling.

And where, in the meantime, was the client?

The guest cabin is only a stone's throw from my own, but the two are hidden from each other by trees and boulders. I stepped over the rocky trail between them; the cabin looked deserted. There was no smoke coming from the chimney; the door was fastened securely; and the shutters were bolted tight against the windows. I pulled open the door—and there the client sat, crouched by the table in the gloom. He was absolutely petrified.

He had been paddling on the lake for most of the previous day (I could well imagine his euphoria in that perfect summer weather: *This is it! The real wilderness! I am finally here!*) and he had decided to leave the canoe in an inlet a few minutes' walk from home. Halfway along the trail back to the cabin, he met the bear.

He couldn't possibly have known at that point that the bear had broken into my place again, but just seeing the bear caused him to panic. He tore back to the canoe, paddled round to the wharf, hauled the boat out of the water, ran back to his cabin and locked himself in.

And there he had stayed for eighteen miserable hours.

He had read every book about the wilderness that he could lay his hands on and I don't doubt that there would have been bear stories in all of them. His home was surrounded by brushy ranchland tight up against the Kootenays and he seemed to know his local wildlife quite well, but apparently bears had never been an issue. The evidence of the first break-in fazed him not one bit. This was a second-hand experience; someone else's concern. To him the wilderness was a starry-eyed vision of Disneyland where everything is picture-book perfect and emotions are inspired by violins. Now his ideal was shattered; his golden dream of the wilderness tarnished. For the first time in his existence, he had known real fear. That four-legged, furry denizen of the bush he had met on the trail had been the first bear he had ever actually encountered in his life.

Like many people, he had been in love with the romance of wilderness rather than the wilderness itself. And I certainly cannot deny that romance constitutes a large part of why I am here. Nature is fascinating, beautiful, and uplifting to the soul. It is exciting, exquisite and miraculous. But it is also dirty, uncomfortable, itchy and cold, full of disinterested murder and terror, unnecessary cruelty, misery and waste. To accept the wilderness you have to understand that both sides are valid, both are part of the intricate relationships that give us our water, air, all life-support systems and sanity. To deny one side of nature is to abrogate the other, and to understand the essence of these natural laws provides insight into our own behaviour as a species. We are part of nature and nature is part of us. To ignore that is to ignore reality, and I am afraid that is what most people do.

# chapter 2

## spinster lake

*Day 2*
*Following breakfast, we depart Williams Lake and we begin*
*our 500 km journey on Highway 20 (200 km are on good gravel*
*road) westward across the broad expanse of the Chilcotin Pla-*
*teau, through the small communities of Riske Creek, Hanceville*
*and Chilanko Forks. A picnic lunch (included) will be savoured*
*in Bull Canyon. By the time we get to Tatla Lake the snowy*
*spires of the Coast Mountains dominate the western horizon*
*and a few miles beyond Kleena Kleene we stop at Nimpo Lake,*
*in time to explore our home for the next two nights before hav-*
*ing dinner (included). Reflecting the uniqueness of this location*
*our accommodations are varied, ranging from motel rooms to*
*chalets to rustic log cabins.*

Extract from an itinerary offered by
Leisure Island Tours, Victoria

About twelve miles south of Nimpo is a large body of water called
Charlotte Lake, big enough to be marked, if not named, on most
maps. This lake is serviced by two separate logging roads, one of
which ends at a disused guest ranch occupied by caretakers. It is here

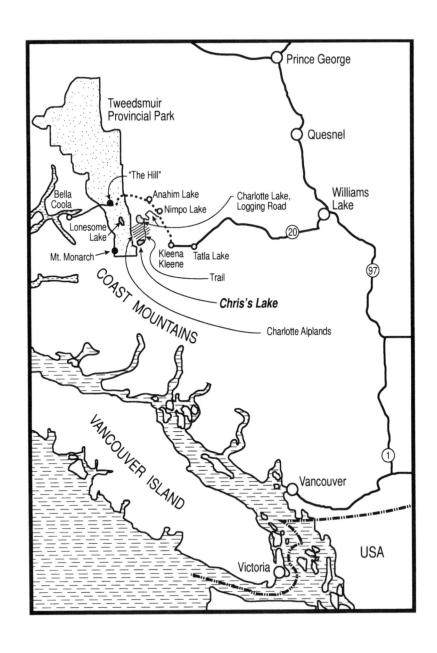

that I leave my truck in summer. My cabins are a further thirteen miles to the south; they lie a thousand feet below the tree line in a high valley of the foothills of the Central Coast Range, pretty much halfway between Nimpo Lake and the southeast corner of Tweedsmuir Provincial Park.

Nimpo Lake supplies my nearest post office (three days a week when the mail comes by truck from Williams Lake), a convenience store, a restaurant, a motel, several resorts and a couple of charter floatplane bases. Anahim Lake, twelve miles along the road towards Bella Coola, is big enough for three stores, another post office and another restaurant, two schools (one on the Native reserve), a clinic, an airstrip (paved six years ago), a hotel, a stampede ground, a police post and underground drunk tank, a trailer that functions as a court-house once every two months and a library six hours a week, more tourist accommodation, and the four, six-hundred-kilowatt diesel generators which provide electricity for the two communities. The next settlement, which is not even big enough for a store, is well over an hour's drive east; in the opposite direction, Bella Coola is reached only after negotiating the spectacular main divide of the Coast Range and dropping down the famous eighteen percent-grade switchbacks known locally as The Hill. North and south of Nimpo is a network of bush roads, but they all peter out within a few miles at ranches and cutblocks. The people scattered loosely around this area are both my neighbours and my stepping stones to the outside world.

I built my cabins single-handedly; because of the roadless location, no heavy machinery could be employed and my tools were not very sophisticated by today's standards: a chainsaw to fall the trees; a come-along and peavey to drag in the logs; ropes, gin poles and a block and tackle to raise them in place. It was, needless to say, a very labour-intensive venture and took the best part of three years (these endeavors are more fully described in *Diary of a Wilderness Dweller*).

Hundreds of the hours I expended in establishing myself involved figuring out and laying down access routes between the cabins and where I would be able to maneuver a vehicle. This location varies depending upon the time of year, for the logging roads are snowmachine-only in the winter and nothing at all when the frost goes out of them in the spring. You will not find my trails on any maps and may, in fact, have extreme difficulty in finding them on the ground for, without constant maintenance, windfalls and brush soon confuse them.

The preferred summer route, which encompasses about ten miles of country above the tree line, is too exposed during much of the winter; the longer, forested route along the river provides the necessary shelter in bad weather but is brushy, swampy and tedious in summer. Then there is a combination route which runs down part of the river valley before climbing to the fringe of the alpine; this is the shortest way to the road but as it traverses the steep north face of a mountain slashed with avalanche chutes, no matter what the other conditions are like, when heavy snow hang on the peaks, it is too dangerous. Each of these journeys has a number of variations depending on the weather or what I want to do or see on the way. The summer hike takes about thirteen hours' steady walking in good conditions and, although I often managed it in a single day when I first came into the country, I am getting older and less enamoured of route marches. In recent years I have taken to spending a night or sometimes two, if either a companion or any trailwork warrants it, en route. In winter I have to walk all the way to Nimpo: the twenty-six air miles are considerably expanded overland. If Charlotte Lake is frozen, it is shorter to go straight across, avoiding the guest ranch where I leave the truck in summer, and connect with the second of the two logging road; nonetheless, the whole trip, most of which has to be completed on snowshoes, generally takes between three and four days.

By far the larger proportion of visitors to my lake arrive by floatplane. This is also the way the bulk of my supplies come in; the flight from Nimpo takes twenty minutes.


My lake is represented by a little blue dot on many maps, even the British Columbia road map, but it is never given a name. Most of the country around here is so little used that it has yet to be catalogued. There are hundreds of lakes in the area and, until recently, mine had very little significance to anyone. Although full of native rainbow trout, the fish are too small to attract the majority of tourist fishermen; there is little feed in the area so it is not a great stopping place

*Chris Czajkowski*

for either large animals or the people who pursue them; it boasts no daunting peaks to climb (these are all farther west) and, despite the spectacular views, it is too far from recognized trails to interest the "in" crowd who flock to whatever wilderness area might be fashionable at the moment. A trapline runs around the lake, but other lakes along it are more significant in some way and, as far as I could determine, the original trapper, Sam Sulin, had no name for it at all.

Different users of the lake over the years have called it whatever they wished and whoever has dealt with those individuals has perpetuated their names. This has had the peculiar result that several titles are in current use.

The present owner of the trapline, Bob Cohen (who bought it from Sam Sulin some thirty years ago), refers to it as Square Lake. On the map it has a shape not unlike a galloping amoeba, but from the surface, in the centre, it has, I have to admit, a kind of squarish look. Bob also calls the next lake upstream Square Lake—they are joined by only a couple of hundred yards of river—but as Bob has a camp on this upper lake, and as his hunting clients are sometimes flown in there, other people call this Cohen Lake.

My lake sits on Whitton Creek, and some people refer to it as Whitton Lake. There are four branches of Whitton Creek and mine has by no means the largest volume of water. This distinction belongs to the southernmost tributary which, however, is so little recognized that on many maps it is missed out altogether. It is traditional to call the largest lake in a system after its river and the biggest lake on all the Whitton Creeks is the next one downriver from mine. Bob always referred to that one as Whitton Lake but from the air it looks like a banana, and due to the increase of flying in latter years, Banana Lake seems to be the most popular name for it and will probably stick.

Nobody seemed to know who Whitton was. I was not particularly keen to live on a lake named after some nonentity, probably a friend of a surveyor sitting on his backside in an office somewhere. But recently, a visitor, on being told that Whitton Creek ran into Charlotte Lake suggested that they must be named for Charlotte Whitton. "Who's she?" I asked. "She was mayor of Ottawa for many years. She was some lady. She caused no end of trouble for all kinds of people." That little bit of history made the idea of Whitton Lake much more attractive as a name.

Avnorth, the floatplane company I use most of the time, calls it Chris Lake; I call it My Lake; and one of the names that has circulated since I first came here is Spinster Lake, in deference no doubt to my solitary nature. I called my hiking business Nuk Tessli, which is the Carrier term for west wind: Carrier is one of the native languages in use in the Anahim Lake area. This wind dominates the area, distorting and twisting the trees and subjecting me and my cabins to some pretty heavy-duty battering at times. I refer to my point by that name, but it is not a name that will come readily to most people's minds so I have not insisted that the lake follow suit. Nuk Tessli can also create strong turbulence in the air above the lake, and the flight-seeing tour operators sometimes refer to the area as "Puke Pass." So you could say that I live at Nuk Tessli, Spinster Lake, Puke Pass— but I think it will be a while before the post office assigns a zip code to that address.

# chapter 3

# bear facts #2

*... I began to relax. It was apparent that few, if any, people or bears were going to molest me. Nevertheless, I kept my .300 Savage rifle and 16-gauge shotgun loaded and a chain on the door at night.*

Anne LaBastille, *Woodswoman*

When Floyd pulled his plane in a curve and headed back towards Nimpo that sunny June day, it might have meant the end of my Kootenay client and his golden dreams of wilderness heaven, but it was by no means the end of the bear.

My old dog Lonesome has been with me right from the beginning of my cabin-building ventures. She has had a considerable number of bear encounters and very early on adopted the policy that discretion was the better part of valour. If, however, she is accompanied by another, more aggressive dog, she will stand her ground quite well and bark—and as bears are the only thing she ever barks at, this trait is quite useful. Partly because of that, and partly because she has carried a little pack for years and I was getting hooked on the idea of having some other creature haul my gear for me, I acquired another mutt. Sport was raised on a ranch not far from Nimpo. He is larger than Lonesome, a yellow dog with a lab's drooping ears and a shepherd's Roman nose and dark shadows on his back. He has a short, but very thick, winter coat and a friendly disposition. He was given to me because "he wasn't a good guard dog" (which was fine by me as a tourist business is no place for an aggressive animal) and "the kids have grown up and he was their dog, really." It was only later that I discovered he was a cattle-chaser and had in fact been heading for a bullet.

Sport's other faults are a predilection for garbage—no outdoor can is safe for miles around—and a total lack of on-chain training. He has never become accustomed to being restrained and when I tie him to keep him away from the trash cans when I am visiting outside, he produces the most heart-rending howls.

But at home in the mountains, he has more than earned his keep. He is a good pack dog, regularly carrying twenty pounds with only momentary dislike and, although he is sorely tempted by caribou, can be called back when he tries to chase them. Like Lonesome, he rarely barks except at bears but, unlike Lonesome, when faced with his ursine cousin, he stands his ground.

After the luckless client had left, both dogs gave voice enthusiastically on several occasions. Although I never caught a glimpse of him, I knew that a bear was still in the vicinity, but he was obviously quite happy to keep out of my way. About two weeks after the break-ins, Avnorth's red plane deposited two more hikers at the wharf early one morning. (This was still quite early for tourists in the mountains for there was yet a lot of snow at higher elevations.) A lawyer and a doctor, the two tourists mostly wanted to do their own thing but had hired me for half a day's guiding to orientate themselves and take them above the tree line. .

Even at that early hour it was hot and brilliantly sunny, but the weather was no longer fresh and invigorating as it had been when I had first arrived. The wind had swung round and, although the air movement was barely noticeable, it was now coming from the east. At the beginning of summer, an east wind almost always means thunder and on that morning, the exaggerated heat, the brassy, mirror calm of the lake, and a thin humid haze that was increasing with the sun's elevation, all pointed towards the inevitable storm. I warned the hikers of this, but they were used to camping and did not mind getting wet; nor did they seem bothered by the news of the bear who would surely be a nuisance in their camp should their paths cross. They were armed with pepper spray and bore a veritable carillon attached to their packs. While it is probably good advice to hikers to carry a bell in bear country, I never do simply because I cannot stand the noise.

There have been some spectacular thunderstorms since my tenure began at Nuk Tessli. The year before, a violent storm had split the heavens only an hour after I had arrived home at the end of the tree-planting season. A day or two later, I climbed towards the tree line to map out a section of trail, and found a sizeable tree split asunder. One riven pillar of ripped and slivered trunk still stood, the other two were flung aside like ninepins. Dozens of smaller shattered, yellow chunks populated the area for fifty yards around. Soil had erupted along the tortured direction of the roots and a boulder, round which roots had entwined, had been cleaved in two. A couple of nearby trees, apparently untouched at the time, soon turned up their toes and died. But there was no fire: even the victim boasted no trace of a scorch mark, the physical scar being the only evidence of the awesome burst of energy.

The route to the tree line took us past this shattered tree, but just before it stands a bluff which makes a fine lookout point; on that sultry July morning, it was up this that we first climbed.

I never tire of this view. Not only my lake but several others are spread below and, behind the shallow walls of the high, wide valley, an impressive array of peaks is evident. All this is my world now, full of the minutiae of memory that is the basis of a sense of belonging.

On this particular day, the sun still shone out of a cloudless sky, but the heat was intense and the haze had thickened to a soggy veil, a greenhouse rag of humidity, the like of which I had never seen outside the tropics. And as we watched, the most extraordinary thing happened. A cloud formed in front of our eyes. Not in the sky, but down over the lake. Instantly, the air began to thicken and collapse inward; at the same time the cloud, white as damp wood smoke, writhed heavenward like a demon possessed. Within seconds it towered over us and began to mushroom while, faster and faster, more air coalesced and spilled to fill the void.

"We'd better get off here," I said, trying to sound calm—a guide, after all, must surely demonstrate complete control of any situation. Packs were hoisted and, like a jangling train of camels, the hikers dutifully fell in behind.

We scrambled off the bluff and re-entered the forest, passing, very quickly, the lightning-struck tree. Our situation was still very exposed for the forest was sparse and the trail wound among rocks and boulders that topped a ridge. The cloud had swelled and greyed the sky, and was already spitting fire and grumbling in a business-like manner. But still it grew and grew; and then the full fury of the storm was unleashed.

Crackling bolts of electricity accompanied by tremendous explosions followed one after the other like a barrage of cannon fire. Hailstones the size of fingernails roared down in a wall of ice. *Oh God!* I thought in terror. *I don't want to be here!* But there was no escape. We simply had to endure. We divested ourselves of everything metal—tents, packs, pepper cans, belts with metal buckles, cameras—left them on the ridge and scrambled down the slope towards as dense a tree as we could muster to at least gain some shelter from the pounding hail. One of the hikers was wearing shorts and his legs were pink with cold and the abrasion from the ice.

It seemed that we stood there forever, saying little, but it might have been no more than half an hour before the hail turned to heavy rain and the thunder had eased to less terrifying proportions. We were soaked to the skin and our main concern now was the cold. Although I offered them the use of a cabin, the hikers still preferred to continue. I took them about a mile farther, to where the trail ended close to the tree line; from here there was a view across a high basin and their route could easily be pointed out. The rain had lightened to a steady drizzle and the air beneath the low roof of cloud was sweet and fresh. I pointed out a few topographical features in relation to their maps and left them to their own devices. The clanking of their carillon trailed flatly into the cool, rainy air as they gradually disappeared from sight. They were due back at the cabin in four days.

The dull, damp weather left by the storm persisted. The wind stayed easterly, and this is significant, for it was this factor which precipitated the next encounter with Mr. Bear.

The cabins sit on a squarish point jutting into the lake, which is three miles long and runs roughly southwest to northeast. When the wind comes from the coast it barrels down the lake and picks up the scents from the cabins, spreading them over the hinterland and alerting any animal of my presence. The east wind does the opposite; it clears the point of human scent and encourages curious animals to come closer. I was now being woken two or three times a night by the barking of the dogs but, although I kept a flashlight handy, any visitor was always gone by the time I stumbled to the door.

Since the break-ins, I had given some thought to the bear's psychology. Although very aware that I was probably not the only person to think I could outwit a bear, I decided to set a trap.

Why had the bear chosen that particular window as his point of entry when I would have thought the door would have been easier to demolish? Probably because a large boulder close to the window gave him access—despite their tremendous physical powers, bears are just like the rest of us; unless they are angry or afraid, they spend some time figuring out the least energy-consuming way to negotiate a problem. The flimsy door did not respond to the first poke with a paw (although the gouge by the bolt is permanent record of his attempt) and so was not as attractive to him as the see-through window. The fact that the first break-in had imploded the glass and the second merely piled it by the sill indicated that he now had the measure of this technological anomaly—and what had worked successfully for him on one occasion would surely be the first thing he would try in the future. So what if I put false divisions across the window and ran from them a string which, when pulled, would activate the trigger of a shotgun whose barrel would end six inches from his nose? I would have to build a strong frame to hold the weapon so that it would not buck when discharged. I would need pulleys to feed the force from a descending paw back to the trigger but could probably make do with the stock of cotton bobbins and fishing reels I had on hand. But if the tension on the string was right and the firearm was pointed correctly (and I crouched on the boulder and reached up like a bear, trying to estimate where the best direction of fire would be), surely the next time the animal came to visit would be his last.

The whole thing was highly illegal of course. But for humans there could be no danger. Because of the roughness of the ground,

no person would ever choose to walk along that side of the cabin, and in any case the gun could be activated only by smashing the false window divisions. There would be no need for any person to come into the cabin that way; the walkway directs human visitors to the door and the door has never had a lock. It is so far from the road that any foot travellers who find this place are unlikely to load themselves with my possessions. It is very rare for persons to come here unless they fly and, whereas there are idiots among plane owners, just as there are in any group of society, the likelihood of a felon appropriating my pretty rocks and sticks and beat-up collection of second hand books is infinitesimally slim. In any case, a locked door would have little purpose. The axes hanging in the porch or a tool the perpetrator himself might bring would make short work of it.

Nonetheless, to make people aware of the trap I drew up two large notices:

> ## DANGER
> **Loaded gun bear trap.**
> **Do not walk past west windows.**

I posted them on the front of the cabin and the door where they would be seen by anyone approaching in either direction. Surely no human who reached this place would be unable to read. (That the bear was literate could not be discounted: during his second break-in he had chomped a Scrabble game which, along with the thesaurus he had chewed on his first visit, proved him to be a bear with a definite fondness for letters: and if an ability to decipher the notice kept him out of the cabin, I asked for nothing more.)

The framework of the trap took so long to put in place I resigned myself to having it as a permanent fixture while the bear remained a nuisance, but the gun was always removed and unloaded while I was home. At night, during the time when the creature was so obviously intent on getting in, I laid the shotgun, broken open with a shell in the breech, on the table beside my glasses, the flashlight and the bear-spray can. Those nights were not particularly restful, for the dogs woke me constantly. It is rare for a bear to enter an occupied cabin, but it has happened and, unlike Anne LaBastille, I had no great faith that, should the bear attempt it, the firearm would be the answer. I had fired the thing only twice, at a tin plate nailed to a tree, when I had bought the gun from a friend. I know I should have practised with it but I hate loud noises and ammunition costs money so I kept putting it off.

The night before the hikers were due to return, the dogs woke me yet again. I had only just dozed off and, despite the overcast, due to the long northern summer day it was almost, but not quite, dark. The dogs were in a frenzy: I grabbed shotgun and flashlight and opened the door. Not twelve paces away (I measured it later) was the bear. He was standing on his hind legs, behind one of the small brushpiles not yet disposed of, furry round ears forward, not at all aggressive, just curious. He looked straight towards me, totally ignoring the dogs; Lonesome had disappeared although she was still barking, but Sport leapt up and down equidistant between me and the bear, yelping joyously, the hair on his shoulders frizzed out with excitement.

We stared at each other. I raised the gun. Should I shoot or shouldn't I? I had been told that a shotgun loaded with a slug was good for fifty yards and this was well within the range. The flashlight's beam twinkled in the bear's small, bright eyes. His fur seemed to have a golden sheen but that could easily have been a trick of the light.

What if I didn't kill him? It was raining quite heavily and dark; if he were wounded I could not hope to track him. And the two hikers were still out there. Would the pepper spray be effective at this distance? Probably not—and what about Sport who was jumping in between? On the porch, I was high enough to shoot over the dog's head but the pepper spray would land right on him. I couldn't very well tell him to hold his nose and run.

The bear had not moved. Surely I could not miss at this range. The cowboy stories I read as a child told me to seat the stock of the gun tight against my shoulder to minimise the kick, and to squeeze, not pull, the trigger. (From what strange sources our knowledge is gleaned!) With the barrel pointing right between the bear's eyes, I fired. The report seemed remarkably quiet. The bear dropped instantly to the ground. And while I was stupidly realizing that the shotgun held only one shell and the rest were still in their box on the table, he heaved himself back to his feet and galloped away. His feet drummed suprisingly loudly on the duff of the trail and his gait told me he was staggering and lurching. But he nonetheless made considerable speed and was rapidly out of earshot.

All I could hear now was the hiss of the rain. I stepped to the brushpile. The flashlight showed a fist-sized lump of coagulating blood on the ground. I had hit him, then. I had a wounded bear, in the dark, in the rain, and two hikers out in the bush due to walk the gauntlet of the point in the morning.

There was nothing to be done that night, but as soon as it was decently daylight, I called Lora at the floatplane base, on the radiophone. "Tell the conservation officer I have wounded a bear and there are two hikers out in the bush," I shouted (reception is not always very good). She asked me to hold on while she called by landphone to Bella Coola, eighty miles west, where the conservation officer was located. I left the radio switched on and she soon came back to me. "It'll be some hours before the C.O. can get there but, weather permitting, he should arrive sometime today." The cloud was still thick but it was patchy and the rain had eased, so it looked like there would at least be some flying weather.

In the meantime I could warn the hikers. If they came down the way I had suggested, they would end their trip by walking around the north shore of the lake. I wrote a note and tucked it in a screw-

*Chris Czajkowski*

top canning jar, then towed the spare canoe to where the trail first ran beside the water. They could not help but stumble over it and by using the canoe they would hopefully avoid the bear.

It was afternoon before one of Avnorth's pilots flew in between showers with the conservation officer. I described what had happened and showed him the blood on the ground—and the fresh two-inch hole in the wrist-thick branch sticking out of the brush pile that daylight had revealed. That was obviously where the force of the bullet had expended itself. The C.O. said that tracking the bear would be impossible now. He agreed that a bear who was bold enough to stand up to a light and a dog was not a very desirable neighbour. "It's likely," he added," that he has received enough of a fright to scare him away. But if you get another chance to shoot him, aim at the body. Head shots are always unpredictable but if you get him in the body, even if you don't kill him right away, sooner or later he will die." With that, he closed his notebook and left.

Later, the hikers arrived home safely, totally unaware of the drama, for they had elected to come down the way we had climbed and had not passed the canoe with its note. They had seen no sign of any bear whatsoever.

It was to be a couple more weeks before the next group arrived and I worked on trails along the next lake upstream, commuting by canoe every day. The trap was religiously activated every time I left the cabin, and I arrived home, squirt can at the ready, with visions of a bleeding hairy hulk draped over my windowsill, but the gun was never fired. In my explorations, I found trees freshly gouged and ripped about six feet from the ground which is a bear's way of marking his territory. Two were close to my own place and several were scattered along the trail. A trap cabin about eight miles away had also been broken into, and trees around it had been similarly marked. All these gouges were sappy and fresh so it was likely they had been made by the same animal. But things had quieted down; the dogs never barked and I assumed that the bear had either died or figured that there were easier pickings elsewhere.

About ten days later, when the showery weather finally quit, I slid the canoe into the new-washed world and paddled to the back of the lake where there was a riotous patch of columbine newly out that

I wanted to try and paint. A couple of concentrated hours were spent there, in complete silence, while the dogs snoozed in the undergrowth nearby. The paddle home was somnolent with heavy, humid sunshine and the dogs trotted quietly along the shore. As I approached the wharf there was a snort; a crash of brush; and a great bellow of barking. There, once more, was the bear. This time, he ignored me completely; his single concern was for Sport. He whirled around, only yards from me as I sat startled in the canoe, and tore to the nearest tall tree. Sport gave joyous tongue and galloped in hot pursuit. As I leapt out of the boat and flung the rope around a cleat I heard the familiar sharp, rhythmic scratching of a bear clawing at bark. When I next saw him he was fifty feet in the air, standing casually on a slim, high branch, chopping his teeth noisily in Sport's direction.

I ran for the shotgun—the cabin was inviolate: thank goodness I had come home when I did—and, pockets stuffed full of slugs, I ran back to the tree. The bear was a large and healthy-looking male with a beautiful, gold-tipped coat. I could see no sign of any previous injury. Once again he lay in my sights. But what would happen if I only wounded him and, despite his fall, he was still active enough to come after me? Would I be able to reload the shotgun in time? The cabin with its protective walls was too far to run. And whereas fifty feet should be close enough for the weapon's range, it was a vertical shot—and there were quite a few branches in the way. I lowered the gun. Perhaps if I backed off and called Sport away, the bear would come down and I would have a better chance at him. But the moment we drew back, the bear whizzed down the tree with the alacrity of a fireman down his pole, and tore off into the bush.

Interestingly, during this encounter, he ignored me completely. His total concentration was on the dog. And yet, during our evening meeting, he had paid no mind to Sport at all despite the dog's proximity. I can only assume that he associated the dog with the blow he had received and it was to Sport that I owed the bear's ignominious retreat.

And where was Lonesome while all this was going on? The canoe was still tied loosely to the wharf and needed to be hauled out of the water. It had drifted to the full length of its painter and stood several feet from the shore. And in it, curled in the smallest possible ball under the furthest seat, was Lonesome.

*Chris Czajkowski*

# chapter 4

## the hunt for the arctic primrose

*"Well, nothing in the world," said Peter, "is intact and precious
and absolutely beautiful: everything is contaminated and mud-
dled and nasty and slimed over and cracked."*

*"Something is good," she said. "Something is. This is." She lifted
up a feather-leaved stem covered with tiny vetch flowers. Each
flower was purple above and blue beneath and very faintly striped
as if the colour had been drawn in by repeated strokes of a very
fine pen.*

*"Oh, nature," said Peter. "I don't count that. That's just stuff."*

Iris Murdoch, *A Fairly Honourable Defeat*

Francie Wilmeth, Bob Cohen's trapping partner, has a mother who
often accompanied them on their month-long, trapline-stocking expeditions, which they usually did on horseback during August. They
would pile firewood by their shelters (normally a rectangular enclo-
sure three logs high over which they would pitch a tent), add flour,
beans and coffee to their caches, and repair any of the depredations
the bear might have made to Sam Sulin's cabins. About twenty years
ago, on one of their earlier trips, Francie's mother collected a few

plants for a friend who worked in a museum. One of these specimens, Bob told me, was an Arctic primrose.

As a child, I often used to think I would have made a good explorer but assumed I had been born far too late; that all the world had
been documented and there was nothing left to discover. How I en-
vied Charles Darwin and his endlessly explorable world. But although
Britain, where I grew up, is catalogued in infinite detail, even there
much is still unknown and in this untouched land I now inhabit, virtu-
ally nothing has been documented. Maps are all based on old aerial
photographs and sporadic surveys done from horseback sixty years
ago; lakes have filled in, rockslides have altered the flow of water and
much of the information is either out of date or ill-recorded in the first
place. When I arrived, the British Columbia Geological Survey had
not yet gone through the area: local pilots knew the country well enough
from the air, but very few people had examined it on foot for more
than a few yards away from wherever a plane could land. Only half a
dozen lakes were big enough for this purpose. Bob, needless to say,
knew his vast area intimately but his prime interests were the animals
he trapped and to which he guided hunters, and he had never bothered
to teach himself much about plants. Not that he failed to notice them—
far from it: he had an amazing botanical directory in his head. But he
did not know what any of them were called and, with the exception of
Francie's mother's few specimens, very little information about plants
had been collated for hundreds of miles in any direction. And those
few surveys that had transpired were the results of small groups flown
into odd places for a week or two by helicopter, a somewhat haphazard
way of making a census.

So what? Isn't one mountain much like another?

Unfortunately, many people, even environmentalists, subscribe
to this fallacy, which illustrates as much as anything why little is known
about alpine ecosystems. As with every other type of ecological niche,
each mountain is unique. British Columbia itself is a concertina of
ranges, all of which were once separate terranes travelling north where
they collided with the North American tectonic plate drifting west.
Although all the terranes were volcanic in origin, several have been
covered by sea and subject to all kinds of weathering and transfor-
mations during their long and ancient journeys, with the consequence

*Chris Czajkowski*

that one range differs greatly in soil type from another. With the recession of the last ice age, peaks within the ranges have become isolated islands, and each has developed its own unique grouping of flora and fauna. I have often found a species in one high creek or on one ridge only, occasionally represented by no more than two or three solitary plants, with not another specimen visible in the whole radius of my wanderings. Furthermore, many species in this harsh and capricious climate flower only when conditions suit; and if they leave little of the plant behind when they are done, it is largely luck which would have the collector in the right place at the right time. The alpine areas of Western Canada, excluding the Rockies and a few locations in the lower mainland, are probably one of the least-studied ecological niches in the world.

I was not aware of this when I chose to live in this area, but a love of both plants and hiking were soon pushed to euphoric heights by the excitement of being an explorer in an unknown land. Since I have been at Nuk Tessli, few activities have delighted more than the prospect of stepping onto an untrodden stretch of alpine country. The news that there were Arctic primrose in the area was particularly intoxicating for I had never seen any of the various species before, not even during a summer spent in the Arctic. Species of plants, like animals, have varying degrees of charisma associated with them; among botanists, *Primulaceae* rank high on the scale. Such an addition to my collection would be a coup indeed.

Meetings with Bob and Francie are sporadic; I might see them once during the summer when their horseback tours happen to coincide with my own ramblings, and perhaps twice in the winter either at their base cabin on Charlotte Lake or, more rarely, at some point along the trapline. At almost every encounter after learning about the primrose's existence, I quizzed them on the location of this exciting plant.

I had no doubt that Bob and Francie knew the exact site but, because very few of the hundreds of peaks, creeks and lakes in the area have names, and because, at that time, I knew so little of the country, their descriptions of how to get there were far from clear. So the information I amassed was: the time of year it was collected (August, for that is when Francie's mother would have been in the country); and "a creek up a valley south of Square Lake, which has a strip of black rock over which the water rushes"; and "it can be found in any north-facing creek." This last assertion puzzled me because all of the primulas were reputed to be uncommon. However, the designation of "north-facing creek" narrowed the field, for the north- and south-facing slopes of all the mountains are very different. Southern aspects are nature's solar collectors. They generally slope gently, are more exposed to wind and ultraviolet bombardment, and snow leaves them quickly. Thus their water supply soon disappears and the species that live there, while able to bloom early, must tolerate considerable drought for the bulk of the year. Indeed, the action of the wind and sun might leave them exposed all winter, in which case the range of plants is even more limited, for they also must have mechanisms to cope with extreme cold and unimaginable wind chill as well as summer dryness and heat.

North faces are steep and shaded; the ice age has never really left them. Permanent snow eats away at the rock, thawing and freezing pries away boulders and leaves broken cliffs and large areas with such a short snow-free season that not even lichens can establish a hold. The snowbanks feed rushing torrents all through the summer. Shade predominates and when the sun's rays do strike, they are more oblique and have less power. This produces a damp, cool and extremely short growing season and the small gravel flats and ledges between the rocks are therefore excellent hunting grounds for more specialized and sometimes rare species.

The first year I attempted to find the Arctic primrose it was mid-August before I could begin. This was late for most of the flowers, but species in north-facing creeks would not yet be shrivelled by the sun and frost and I set off with great anticipation. Not that I necessarily expected to come upon the primrose at once, but most of the country was still new to me and the valley south of my own was territory I had yet to explore. Until recently, I had not possessed the topographical map of this area; in the end, I had been obliged to write to Ottawa for it.

I hiked up to the river crossing (the bridge was not then in place) and bush-bashed for most of a day up the southern branch of Whitton Creek. At the head of the first of several lakes as the country opened up was a classic north-facing stream tumbling and roaring from a small glacier high against the steep dark wedge of Wilderness Mountain. "In every north-facing creek," Bob had said—I would give it a go. The creek was brushy below but a short scramble up it revealed an unexpected magnificence. Choking every available piece of solid ground between the flashing, rushing skeins of leaping, sunlit water were floods of rich rose-purple and yellow. The first was the ubiquitous mountain fireweed which grows in such startlingly lush mats in any snow-fed seepage, often far beyond the limits of other plants. The yellow was a combination of mountain arnica and water-spangled clumps of a dwarf monkeyflower of a richness of hue equalled only by summer farm butter. Buried damply among the other plants were the almost petal-less *Stelleria umbellata* and the fairy-like, red-anthered stars of the red-stemmed saxifrage, one of the commonest of eleven members of that genus that I had so far recorded in the area. Ignoring the horseflies who buzzed round my head with a vengeance, I sat surrounded by the shout of the creek and the dazzle of colour and

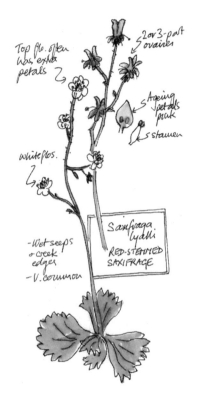

*Top flo. often has extra petals 2*

*2or 3-part ovaries*

*Ageing petals pink*

*stamen*

*white flos.*

*Wet seeps of creek edges*

*V. common*

*Saxifraga lyalli*
*RED-STEMMED SAXIFRAGE*

sketched and photographed the monkeyflower and the *Stelleria* to add to my collection. (Herbariums have asked me to press specimens, but if the plant is common and well-known, I cannot see that is necessary and, if it is rare, I would rather leave it to struggle along undisturbed. Besides, each institution wants its own herbarium and visits to them have shown me vast piles of undigested material which it takes an eternity to catalogue; occasional specimens of my own have languished in the "in" cabinets for years but have still not been entered into the record.)

However, this creek, wonderful though it was, had nothing resembling the black rock strip that Bob had described, or any member of the primrose family, and I continued west along the valley, checking every north-facing trickle en route plus any other ecological niche that looked interesting. At the west end of Wilderness Mountain was a moraine wall. These are usually barren here, apart from lichens, as all soil and gravel washes away from between the rocks. However this one was quite different. It hid a lake and glacier until I climbed onto it so the spectacular view was unexpected. The lake half-filled the basin; old and seamed ice plunged straight into the water (there was even a little iceberg floating free) and at the dry end of the basin the ice sloped so gently onto a sandy plateau that it was possible to creep into the dripping blue-green caves under the snout of the glacier or walk without difficulty onto the broad roadway of the ice itself. As if that was not enough, the mile-long moraine wall produced the medallion-like dwarf hawksbeard, seen only in the Arctic before; *Erigeron humilis*, the Arctic daisy; and an unusually long-rayed *Erigeron compositus*, all hanging precariously by the tips of their root hairs in that high and splendid world.

But of an Arctic primrose, there was no trace.

The next time I saw the trapper family was the following winter when their work brought them close to my cabin and they stopped by for a visit. This was opportune for I was able to dig out the map and ask them exactly from which creek the specimen had been collected. "Right there," Bob said, stabbing his gnarled finger among the vapid topo-map colours.

I had been hunting for it in the wrong valley.


With the August of the following year full of commitments, I could spare only a couple of days in mid-July on my quest. The destination Bob had indicated proved to be a fairly easy hike from home and I was making camp by the middle of the afternoon at the point where "Primrose Creek" left the confines of a narrow, dark, snow-walled gully and spilled out onto a wide alpine shelf, giving me a sunny, gentle platform from which to view a great panorama of the Coast Range. A wonderful spot to lounge and look, but the lure of the primrose was too strong and I plunged forthwith into the gully. The creek was at once tortured and roiling, and singing with snowmelt roar. I climbed up slippery, mossy rocks step by step, the water's confined bellowing bouncing off the granite walls. At every bend a new aspect of the creek was revealed and soon there appeared a slab of dark rock which answered Bob's description. However, I was too early in the year. The growing season in this high valley was so compressed that the timing to catch the plant in flower would be crucial. There were the usual wet-shade-loving saxifrages and *Epilobium* species, but all the plants were still tightly in bud and I could not identify them all; the rock slab itself was almost completely buried in snow, the water rushing from a blue-ice tunnel at its foot.

So it was not until the third summer that I reached "Primrose Creek" at what would probably be the optimum time to catch the plant blooming. The canyon which housed the creek was perhaps a mile long but, due to its steepness and narrowness, there were not a great many places where anything could grow. And I explored every one of them, inch by inch, particularly the infamous black rock slab. I swear I looked at every single plant in the place. I found sticky onions and creeping azaleas, heathers and *Senecios, Erigerons,* paintbrushes, grass of parnassus and saxifrages. If a primrose was growing there, surely I would have seen it.

Doubts began to set in.

In my conversations with Bob and Francie, I came to realize that, despite their great knowledge of the country and its plants, their taxonomy was hardly textbook material: they had once described to me, for instance, a "snow orchid" which turned out to be a type of fireweed. But the person to whom the primrose had been sent had been a colleague of Francie's late archeologist father; they had apparently worked in the same museum. Surely that source would be reliable and be able to confirm the specimen's authenticity. Perhaps it was one of those plants which did not bloom every year. Or perhaps it was just my inexperience that failed to bring it to light. But maybe there was a more ominous reason for the plant's elusiveness. Had the Arctic primrose been rare, and did its collection and subsequent removal from the site mean that it was now, for my locality, extinct?

I wondered if Francie's mother's friend of twenty years ago was still alive.

Unfortunately, both the trapping family's itinerant habits and my lack of quick means of communication meant that it might be some time before I would see Francie and be able to trace this friend. I seemed to remember that the museum where she had worked was in Ottawa; as I had botanical contacts living there, I first sought their help. But the Ottawa herbarium's plants were labelled only "British Columbia" and without the collector's name we were stumped. When I finally tracked Francie down, I asked her to ask her mother to ask the friend … and after a while the name of a person was forwarded to me, not from Ottawa, but the Museum of Anthropology in Montreal. The exploration through the archives was becoming almost as intriguing as the search for the plant in the field.

In due time a letter came from Montreal.

The specimen collected had not been a primrose at all.

It was nothing but the common old red-stemmed saxifrage.

Bob had been right, it was in any north-facing creek. It was, in fact, smothering the black rock slab. The mistake had been understandable as, according to the photocopied herbarium sheets sent to me by my informant, *Primula cuneifolia* looks superficially similar to *Saxifraga lyalli*, particularly in its leaf shape and arrangement. And primroses are pink and saxifrages are white—right? Except that *Saxifraga lyalli* often turns pink with age, a fact that is never recorded in field guides. A closer examination of the flower's structure was the only clue to its identification.

Will I ever discover an Arctic primrose in this area? The possibility is slim for it likes calcareous soils and these are few and far between in this great wall of coastal granite. But there are odd pockets of ancient limestone in one or two places in the area so if all conditions come together, its existence is not completely out of the question.

But the expeditions had otherwise been far from unproductive. On a dampish gravel flat, right on the tree line and close to where the creek erupts from its narrow cut, I discovered a tiny plant no more than an inch high. It had a clump of light green basal leaves and two or three naked stalks supporting three white, four-petalled flowers each the size of a grain of wheat. There were perhaps a dozen insignificant specimens scattered through an area the size of a city lot. Hardly spectacular, but I could not find it in any of my books and it was to be another plant that gave me a lot of pleasurable archive-hunting before it was identified. That it was a gentian was apparent by its structure, but it was three years before I could finally put a name to it. And *Gentianella tenella,* tiny and insignificant though it might seem, has (outside Mt. Fairweather on the Alaskan border) never been recorded in British Columbia before. So I might not have found my Arctic primrose—but I still had my coup.

Primrose Ck
27 July 95

Gentianella
tenella

# chapter 5

# *squirrel squeak or squirrel-speak*

*In the Koran, Allah asks, "The heaven and earth and all be-*
*tween, thinkest thou I made them in jest?" ... If (the creature)*
*was not made in jest, then was it made in earnest?*

Annie Dillard, *Pilgrim at Tinker Creek*

Bears are not the only creatures to attempt to infiltrate my dwelling.
White-fronted deer mice appear in endless cycles of population explosions—sometimes the traps are full every night for weeks and then,
without much warning, there is not so much as a rustle for the next
month or two. I bought Warfarin for the mice once, but find even
this "safe" chemical suspect. The regular spring-loaded traps are as
good an answer as any. They are efficient and painless for the most
part, and eminently recyclable. Trapping mice live and packing them
to a new location is as cruel as having them die of shock and starva-
tion in sticky cardboard tunnels—no prey animal will survive long in
the wild without the safety of familiar harbours and its last hours will
be an agony of terror. Other small rodents—I'm not sure if they are
voles or lemmings—are seen less but are probably just as numerous;
they are the primary agents responsible for the random tooth marks
on the vegetables in the root cellar. Shrews pop up occasionally

through the wider gaps between the homemade floorboards, especially if I am butchering and they smell the meat, but they are probably more helpful than otherwise as they are voracious carnivores and eat large insects as well as rodents if they get a chance.

It is while I am away for long periods, either tree-planting or doing the rounds of the craft fairs in the fall, that most of these animals make themselves at home. Once I arrived back in the spring to find three bags of dog food completely ruined. They had been up in the attic, but in the outer part away from the rest of my food. The paper covering of one had been ripped from end to end, not chewed as a rodent might have done, and the uneaten kibble had been crushed to powder and distributed over much of the attic. The other two bags had been used as a bathroom to such an extent that the contents were soaked and mouldy and had to be ditched. I was a little mystified at first as to who the perpetrator might be for the kibble was the cheap kind consisting mostly of cereal. The scale of the damage was such that I even entertained thoughts of a wolverine for a while, (they are rare here although occasionally seen) but a wolverine would not have balked at the inner attic's flimsy door or the thin metal skins of the garbage cans which held the bulk of my chewables. In the evening, even before I caught a glimpse of the sharp eyes framed by chestnut fur and the dark, bushy tail, a bad-tempered snarling identified a marten. He did not seem particularly frightened and I hoped he would stay and help control the rodents but after a day or two he went his way.

Packrats are not a common invader; the higher cabins seem largely immune to them although a young one once galloped through this one with about as much finesse as a herd of stampeding horses for a few nights before I caught him. I have never liked killing all these uninvited guests and would be perfectly happy to live with them if they did not make life so uncomfortable. I have little patience with those who move into an area that is totally unsuitable for whatever project they envision such as sheep farming in country where large predators abound, and then blame the indigenous inhabitants for their livestock losses. If I had built my cabins with greater attention to craftsmanship (and more expense) I could probably have kept the little critters out. However, a point is reached when the destruction of my cabin becomes either too costly or even a hazard and, I argue with myself somewhat guiltily, the unseasonable warmth and food I have provided for these small animals have encouraged them to breed more frequently than nature would have allowed, therefore a certain amount of culling is justified. This argument smacks of "wildlife management" policies that are often only an excuse to extract more short-term money from the wilderness and I don't like myself any better for it. I am, at least, selective as an exterminator—the shotgun trap, for instance, will affect only the problem bear and then only if he tries to climb into the cabin—and my executions will have no effect on the animals' habitat which is a far more serious ecological disaster than the death of a few individuals.

For all the bear's propensity for demolition, he did not head the list as the most destructive creature to enter my cabin. That distinction was held by a squirrel. Late one summer, after I had returned from a few days on a plant-hunting trip, I was happily enjoying the calm and peace of the fading light on the lake beyond my window, when I heard one of these little animals scrabble jerkily, in the peculiar way that squirrels do, around the cabin under the eaves. This was not too unusual so my brain only half registered the fact, but the next moment the scampering was only inches from my head, *inside the walls.*

When I built the cabins at Nuk Tessli, two main things dictated the choice of construction methods; one was the lack of tall, straight trees at this altitude and the other was the physical constraints of both the location and myself. So the *pièce en pièce* style of building seemed appropriate. This is based on the old European concept of half-timbered houses where the space between fundamental uprights is filled with whatever material is available; in this case it was more trees but they could be made into short lengths and laid horizontally between the verticals.

For the first building, which is now a guest cabin, I used solid logs for the infill. For the second, in an effort to save trees both from an aesthetic point of view and from the enormous work that falling, trimming, hauling and clearing up after each one entailed, I decided to use half logs for the outside fillers, store-bought boards for the inside and stuff the gap with fibreglass.

It was a big mistake.

It would have worked if my craftsmanship had been of a better standard but I have neither the patience, finesse nor the tools for fine carpentry. The trees from which I coerced both the half-logs for the walls and the boards for the gable ends were green, stunted, twisted and knotty. Consequently they shrank and warped enormously, and the result was a plethora of small gaps and holes which expanded as the cabin dried out. My fine-furniture-making family would throw up their hands in horror at this crude joinery, but it suited the little animals very well. Here was easy access to a wonderful supply of high-tech nesting material, far superior to the grass and bark fibres of tradition, to be had for the simple exercise of chewing. A few mice could be tolerated without too much loss of insulating power, but the squirrel was a whole different ball game. Almost before my astonished brain had time to register his presence within the wall, this particular animal had reached the kitchen area, turned around once in its comfy pink nest, and was silent. I wondered at first if my ears had been deceiving me for there was not a rustle all night and a wooden cabin is such an efficient sounding box that all noise is magnified and sometimes difficult to place. Perhaps he had merely been running outside the walls. But in the morning, just as I was about to blow out the lamp, there was a muffled stirring behind the kitchen shelves, a rapid, reversed thumping close to my head, a scrabbling at the gable end and a final triumphant chirring as the squirrel announced his emergence to the strengthening dawn. I rushed outside to try and spot him, but by the time I pounded round that end of the house, he was gone.

Come full daylight, I dragged the heavy, homemade ladder round to the gable end and had a look. Sure enough, the gap around one of the ill-fitting notches had a rubbed, well-used look and was fringed with several squirrel-coloured hairs. The gable ends were hollow-walled—the flat ceiling of the main room and only the lower walls had been insulated—and, once inside the gable walls, it would not be difficult for the squirrel to find a way lower down. His access hole, however, was easy to block and I jammed wood into another, smaller one while I was at it, thinking that the problem had been solved.

That evening as I was ready to light the lamp again, the jerky scrabble and nasal groaning, with which the squirrel accompanies many of his procedures, started at the usual end of the cabin, continued under the eaves and, while I listened somewhat complacently, reached the newly blocked hole. With barely a pause, there was a further scampering across the gable end, a clattering inside the walls by my head, the comfortable bed-making routine behind the kitchen shelves, and silence. (At least, to give him his due, he never made any noise at night, which is more than can be said about the mice.)

More ladder-lugging and hole blocking ensued. But the following evening, in he went as usual. This continued for several days, with me blocking more and more gaps and becoming more and more puzzled and frustrated. I was beginning to get pretty mad. A squirrel would rapidly make a much bigger hole in the insulation than the mice ever could or, as would surely happen when it got too cold for him to stay in the walls and he went to live in his midden beneath the balsam fir just behind the cabin, he would pack considerable quantities of the stuffing along with him. I took to eating supper outside, swatting blackflies in the dusk, until I finally saw his entrance point at the gable's very peak. My ladder would not reach that far until the snow lay four feet deep on the deck. The only solution was to rip out the interior attic wall and block his efforts with small-meshed wire from the inside. Was he ever annoyed when he discovered that. I could hear him twanging it like a guitar string and swearing up a storm. It kept him out for a while, but I went away again for a few days and when I returned, fresh holes had been chewed in another part of the wall. Having discovered this very Hilton of accommodation, the squirrel would eat through almost anything to get at it; as fast as I blocked one gap, another would appear.

At first, apart from the knowledge of the damage, the episode had seemed in the nature of a game. During the day, while I worked at the woodpile, it was easy to assume the squirrel reciprocated, for the little critter would fling cones onto the roof of the woodshed, flit provocatively through the gaps between the split stove-lengths, and groan and chatter at me from an upright, barely an arm's-length away, fixing me with his pale-rimmed eye. (I am talking about the Douglas squirrel here, not the "fat cat" black squirrels of Ontario and the city parks of Vancouver.) But as the war escalated, I began to realize that the squirrel was in deadly earnest. His persistence was extraordinary. After being foiled with the wire, he never came back at dusk but, several times during the day, he scrabbled round various parts of the walls examining the joints and staring in through the windows. If I was inside, we would eye each other speculatively, mere inches apart, separated only by that piece of glass. (Oddly enough, he never figured out how easy it would be to chew through mosquito netting. The kitchen window is open most of the time in summer—I have even occasionally forgotten to close it when I have been away on a trip, but the squirrel never yet broached the screen.)

And it all started me thinking more about my disrespectful neighbour. I had long been familiar with a good many of his habits: his tree-top nest of grass in summer; his cone-harvesting techniques; the huge, ancient middens where he stores food and sleeps during the winter; his habit of packing mushrooms and even dead mice onto branches and crotches of trees to dry before taking them underground; his acrobatics and vociferations that make me laugh. But there were a lot of things I didn't know. How many squirrels shared the midden? How deep was it? How many young did they have? Did both parents help in the rearing of the offspring? How advanced were the babies when they were born? When were they born? How long were they dependent on their parents?

And there are a couple of things about the squirrel that make him extraordinary. Firstly, what other animal in the world has been designed to gallop headlong down a vertical plane and stop dead? By observing his dizzying peregrinations through his three-dimensional world as closely as possible, I have come to the conclusion that it is the hip joints that absorb the shock of his descent, rather than his front end, but even so, it is a masterly defiance of gravity unparalleled elsewhere in the animal world.

The other remarkable feature of a squirrel's nature is the very one which makes him familiar to us. It is his obviousness. What other wild creature makes such an intentional racket or lives his daily life so demonstrably? Songbirds, for instance, might make a lot of vocal noise during the breeding season, but they are physically a lot more elusive than squirrels. Mice, too, can make a great commotion while they move about a house, but the instant they feel threatened, they are silent. Even the African elephant for all its bulk, and the grizzly bear for all its potential ferocity, move more quietly through their environments than does the squirrel. Only a human can possibly equal such domestic ostentation and that, presumably, is because we now inhabit a world whose dangers bear no relationship to stealth—walking quietly, for instance, does not stop us from being run over by a bus.

Why doesn't the squirrel conform?

It is not as though he doesn't have plenty of natural enemies. Martens live on squirrels and there are so many of them that they are the prime fur crop in these parts. A lucky trapper might take a hundred in a season. Yet martens, who surely have a much better defense than their prey, are so secretive that I might see one once every two years. Once I heard a great crash in a tree and looked up to see a large hawk standing on a branch, empty-footed, realigning his severely ruffled feathers; the hitherto almost continuous squirrel noise was suddenly silenced. Then there are grizzly bears. One of the local middens was dug up like a potato field. The bear might have been primarily after the oil-rich pine seeds that the squirrels had stored there, but I've no doubt a rodent appetizer would have been just as welcome a reward.

So why is the squirrel different? What is going on in my erstwhile neighbour's head while he stares at me from the upright of the woodshed? (Some of the intensity of the gaze may be shortsightedness: I've noticed that they need to go very close to the ends of a branch to see whether or not they carry cones.) A squirrel's antics (when he is not wrecking the house) make us laugh. It is easy for us to assume the squirrel is friendly, cranky, funny. He is, of course, bent primarily on survival and anthropomorphism is frowned on by scientists, but is there not room for something more than logical data and instinct in that small animal's brain? I am enraptured by sunsets and reflections in the lake, for instance, but I don't know why I enjoy them. And if there are no guidelines to define these intangibles for humans, how can anyone itemise such abstractions for other animals? And is the anthropomorphic interpretation of squirrel-speak complete nonsense? Cross-species communication is common enough—many ungulates, for instance, know when a predator is hunting them and will feed calmly in their enemy's presence if he is not. Warning cries are universally understood by any creature with ears and every mother's special call to its young is unequivocally gentle. Even humans, taught that rationality and instinct are incompatible, have no trouble translating the message behind the voice and body language of an angry dog. So perhaps the squirrel's apparent fooling is more than meaningless chatter. Perhaps nature needs a clown.

I had to kill him in the end. I did the deed with a small leg-hold trap but placed bait directly on the pan so that the jaws snapped his neck, a device I find effective for animals of that size. The previous winter had been a mild one, but I knew if we got a spell of forty below I would be crouching beside the stove and burning excessive amounts of firewood. As it was I had often sat at my work table, which is rather a cool spot, with my legs encased in a sleeping bag.

The following fall, as soon as the last tourist left, I moved into the guest cabin and ripped the entire interior of the main one apart. As all the furniture was built-in and nailed to the walls, it was a considerable undertaking. Behind the cottonwood panelling were hundreds of mouse nests and, behind the stove, huge areas where the insulation was missing entirely; no wonder the draughts had whistled. I contemplated digging up the midden under the balsam fir to see what I could retrieve, but the current crop of squirrels seemed so far benign and if I disturbed them they might all move in with me. It took two weeks to block the thousands of mouse-sized holes with rodent wire and, when that ran out, scraps of roofing tin, used canning jar lids (I knew they would come in handy some day) and whatever else I could find. Finally I replaced and added to the insulation and began the laborious process of fitting the interior walls and furniture back together. I didn't doubt the mice would squeeze in again eventually, but if I could keep the squirrels at bay I would be happy. So far, these efforts seem to have worked.

So when, a couple of years after the walls were redone, I found a squirrel running around inside the cabin when I came home after tree-planting in the spring, I was appalled. I did not waste time attempting to see where it had got in, but trapped it right away. As I tossed the warm body to the dogs, I saw, rather sadly, that it was a female with a row of swollen teats. She must have had a nest of babies somewhere. The spring cabin clean-up revealed a fresh-chewed hole under the bed; she had entered through the crawl space and did not appear to have violated the precious insulation, so that, at any rate, was a relief. Had I known that I would at least have attempted to deter her in some other way.

A few days after the event, a plane flew in bearing my summer's supplies and Janis and Markus, a couple of young Germans who were going to help me bring in some firewood. Neither had any experience with chainsaws, but there was nothing wrong with their muscle power so I felled and bucked up the trees while they split and manhandled the stove-lengths. Being an early riser, I generally breakfasted and was away before the young men had eaten, and consequently needed lunch earlier as well. As they did not particularly want the chainsaw whining while they laboured, the arrangement was to the benefit of all.

It was early afternoon and a light rain was falling. All at once, Janis and Markus came running excitedly from the cabin carrying a small, white bucket. "A rat! A rat!" they exclaimed.

Quivering in the bottom of the bucket, its fur matted with the rain, was a baby squirrel.

"Where did you find it?" I asked

"In the wool by the door," they replied, somewhat obscurely.

I should have thrown it to the dogs there and then, but of course

I had to try and feed it. Back at the cabin I soaked a rag in a little warm milk (a container of which had come in on the plane) and was rewarded by a few sporadic swallows. All of a sudden there was a small wheezing noise and a little plop, and a second baby squirrel landed on the floor. It had come from a shelf jammed with hats and gloves above the coats by the door. This, then, was "the wool." I had been hearing a few odd noises in that direction but had thought it was mice in the ceiling. Further investigation showed a third baby in a nest of garments so thoroughly chewed they had been felted into a solid ball.

They had to be the offspring of the mother I had killed—it was certain that no other squirrel had been in the cabin since. But the extraordinary thing was that these babies had survived for over a week without anything to eat or drink. A human would have succumbed long before.

All three managed to down a dribble or two of milk, but two did not last out the day. The third, which was the one my visitors had found, began to show a little more liveliness. Her eyes were still closed and her tail was ratlike with only a short fuzz of hair. She could not walk very well but whether this was just her normal state of development or due to her deprivation I had no means of knowing. I put her nest into the little bucket and moved it to the shelf behind the stove where I figured it might be warmer. She soon learned the smell of her milky rag and would happily clutch it with her amazingly long, articulated fingers. I called her Cleopatra because after every feed she was bathed in milk. The digits on all four of her feet were remarkably well developed. During this time there were still snow patches around the cabin and as one of these melted, the carcass of a flying squirrel was exposed. A small group of these pretty animals had hung about my place for a time during the winter—also attracted by dog food. Why this one had died was not apparent, but it had been perfectly preserved in the snowdrift. It was interesting to contrast its tiny, underdeveloped paw with Cleopatra's remarkably attenuated toes.

Although the other two squirrel babies died, Cleopatra was by no means the only survivor of the orphaning. She was infested with an astounding number of fleas and lice. The fleas were chocolate brown and of such a large size that they might be compared to a mouse on a human—imagine having twenty or thirty of those jumping about on you as well as a couple of dozen coaster-sized lice. Several of these did in fact jump about on me for a while—I got quite a few bites—but Cleopatra's frequent bathings, both with the milk and a wet rag afterwards, served to make the parasites abandon ship.

Or perhaps they were foretelling the inevitable. Cleopatra, I am afraid, was doomed. After about a week, I ran out of liquid milk and tried to feed her with reconstituted powder. She succumbed the next day. It seemed a paradox to kill the adults on the one hand and try and feed the babies on the other, but that, I suppose, is one of the idiosyncrasies we have forged for ourselves as affluent human beings.

# chapter 6

# *rhythms and woodshed blues*

*It is a matter of surprise to many persons to see the great amount of energy of mind and personal exertion that women will make under the most adverse circumstances in this country. I have marked with astonishment and admiration acts of female hero-ism, for such it may be termed in women, ... (as they) perform tasks from which many men would have shrunk. ...they have reso-lutely set their own shoulders to the wheel, and bourne the burden with unshrinking perseverence unaided; forming a bright exam-ple to all around them, and showing what can be done when the mind is capable of overcoming the weakness of the body.*

Catherine Parr Traill, *A Canadian Settler's Guide*

The short summer with its urgent flowering and burgeoning seeds is gone; the flames of autumn have flickered and died. The lake is a mirror, the mountains freshly whitened and the remaining, withered alder leaves along the waterfront are bejeweled with frozen diamonds like harridans whom nobody has told that the party is over.

It is cranberry-picking time.

The fall at Nuk Tessli, although sometimes little more than a rain-sodden rag between storms, is, at its best, a prolonged orgy of colour asprawl through limpid September days. The area is too high and harsh to support large deciduous trees—even the aspen balks at the conditions up here—but the underbrush, the plants that will be protected by snow most of the winter, squander a no-less-brilliant palette. The burnt sienna of the sedges in the meadows vibrates against the deep ultramarine of the ponds and lakes. Mountain rhododendrons blaze red, bronze and gold; willows turn yellow, squashberries flaunt purple; the Labrador tea's bottom leaves become a bold orange that is the antithesis of its upper, olive foliage; and the huckleberries burn with crimson fire. Scientists tell us this feast for the eyes is simply the result of vegetative garbage disposal. Energy reserves are withdrawn into storage and waste products are channelled into the leaves before the plant seals itself away from them for the winter. But why should colour be such an issue here? There is no apparent reason for this licentiousness of hue. Colour is a device nature uses to attract pollinators and mates; or to form bonding between species; or to enlist carriers to distribute seeds encased in fleshy fruit. But nothing with eyes will eat these leaves and as an advertisement for procreation this colour is wasted. Only a select number of creatures in fact will be aware of the pageant at all. Birds and insects detect colour—insects can register an even wider spectrum than ourselves, for many of the alpine flowers which look white to us have a variety of pollinator guide-lines that reflect ultra-violet light visible to arthropods. But most mammals are colour-blind. Humans are the only ones to possess the cone cells in the eyeball which send colour signals to the brain; presumably this ability evolved to help compensate the emerging hunter/gatherer for the inadequacy of his other senses. At what stage in the evolutionary story were humanoids graced with a facility hitherto lavished only on insects and birds? And if the sole purpose of an ability to distinguish colour has developed as a means to help us separate a fruit from a leaf, why are we so moved by it? Why does colour constitute one of the primary manipulators of our emotions?

High-bush cranberries, also known as squashberries, are the last of the wild fruits to ripen; indeed they taste a lot better after the frost has been at them. If left alone, they hang on the bushes through the winter; however, if I want them before the other animals eat them, I gather them around Thanksgiving. The plants like wet feet but must be at the edge of their range up here for they inhabit only one or two sheltered patches along a creek and a few wet seepages. The bushes have lost their leaves at picking time and the red berries glow like ruby lanterns among the tangle of winter-brown, sitka alders who are the creek's principal guardians. I have cleared a trail alongside the creek—it is part of my northern route into the alpine— but it avoids the thick vegetation where the berries grow and to pick them it is easier to walk in the creek-bed itself. The water is at its lowest at cranberry-picking time, enabling me to rock-hop dry shod between rills and tiny pools choked with fallen yellow willow leaves, which tremble on the surface film as lightly as an oriental brushstroke. Sometimes there is wet, early snow on the bushes and the moss on the water-washed rocks beneath my feet glows neon green; then I harvest the fruit in rain gear with fingers icy and numbed.

Highbush cranberries contain a large, flat seed so are best made into juice or jelly. They are designed to be eaten and passed through a digestive tract for distribution so although I don't go quite all the way to duplicate nature, I take the seedy pulp and scatter it back along the banks of the creek. Despite the name cranberry, they are not related to the species which is used commercially (and which also grow in one or

-leaves fuzzy to touch: speckled underneath

— late summer

Soopalalie

two places here although not in harvestable quantities) but the taste is similar. Up here, they are one of the few berries which grow in sufficient numbers to be picked and preserved.

Another berry occasionally common enough to gather is the soopalalie, known back east as the buffalo berry. It is much more common lower down on the dry, interior Chilcotin plateau. It was a favoured food of the native people who whipped it up into a froth. It was dubbed "Indian ice-cream" by settlers, but even when they added sugar, as most of natives now do, few settlers enjoyed it. The flavour of the berries is certainly unusual, with a peculiar, bitter aftertaste, but after years of nibbling I find I am growing to like

*Chris Czajkowski*

them. They are also much improved by a frost—freezing turns starches to sugars and sweetens most things—but usually long gone by then as they are an early ripener and bears love them. Bears also eat huge amounts of crowberries, another very common fruit of which the natives gathered a great deal, although probably more out of necessity than preference as it is seedy and does not have much of a flavour. In the fall, bears' scats are full of the apparently barely digested berries. It always amazes me how a large animal with such an enormous energy requirement can not only subsist on these tiny items of food but also seem to pass them through his system largely untouched.

Raspberries, thimbleberries and dewberries exist but they do not bear ripe fruit. The mainstay of my berry crop is the huckleberry. Even so, conditions have to be right for a good harvest, and this might happen only one year in five. They are ready in late August, just about when the black flies begin their quest for blood. Dozens of different species of black fly exist and the one that is the most nuisance here starts biting after the first frost. These annoying little bloodsuckers must be tolerated during picking time but they should not be cursed too readily. Despite the profusion of the huckleberry genus all over the northern hemisphere, the main pollinator of the little hanging flowers, many of which have a constricted mouth, is not known. Ants of all sizes crawl in and out, so they do their part, but even in years when *Formicidae* seem to be busy, vast acreages of bushes will be completely without fruit; the ants, presumably, have a limit on the distance they will travel from their bases. The plants are almost always laden with flowers, but obviously the timing of the blossom and the emergence of the pollinator is crucial. One theory cites some species of black fly as the principal fertilizing agent; who knows? Like ants who farm aphids for their honeydew or make compost heaps to cultivate mushrooms, perhaps black flies are growing huckleberry gardens especially to attract warm-blooded animals to provide them with the blood feast they need to reproduce!

Another species of huckleberry, the mountain blueberry (*Vaccinium caespitosum*), has an equally delicious but completely different flavour. However, it hugs the ground and is so small I gather it only when I am out for a walk, picking a handful then throwing the whole lot into my mouth for a delectable explosion of taste. This species is common

−fall

above the timberline and, in a fruitful year, when it loses its leaves, dense patches of tiny, mauve berries mist the tundra. They must provide a good supply of winter fodder for the small animals that live under the snow.

The turning of the season brings a sense of urgency to another task that demands a lot of my time—bringing in the winter's wood. Eulogies have been written about the merits and joys of dealing with nature's "free" fuel: have you noticed that they are always written by men? Men, moreover, who do not need wood as their sole, year-round energy source for both cooking and heating—and men, what is more, who can drive pickup trucks right to their woodshed door.

Admittedly, the splitting part (the bit that is usually praised) is the least onerous and, providing it is done in small bursts, can be quite a pleasant excercise. Clean, yellow, smooth-grained wood pops rhythmically and musically apart into tidy sizes, while mountain chickadees wheeze in the balsam firs behind the woodshed and a few lazy flakes of snow drift onto a pristine world from a dove-grey winter sky.

I wish.

With no roads, no trucks, and no excess testosterone, filling the woodshed is a dreaded chore. As was the case with the building logs, it is the hauling that constitutes eighty percent of the labour; every single chunk must be moved by muscle power alone. Not just once, but at the very least, three times. On top of which, to complicate matters, I don't always do things the easiest way.

Visitors who have no experience at all of my kind of life might marvel at my monuments, but simply accept that they are somehow conjured into place. It is the people who have done some bush living or cabin building who ask: "Where did you get your logs from?" This compliment for the apparent absence of logging activities is no accident but the product of a lot of hard work. Admittedly, as no vehicles were involved, there was far less damage to the surroundings than there would have been otherwise. The single passage of a Cat would have left a far greater mark on the landscape than all my other logging activities put together.

Second to vehicular abuse, there is no more hideous reminder of the desecration of a forest than severed trunks with their accusing rictus of slivers. When I built my first cabin near Lonesome Lake, I felled the trees from around the cabin site with little idea of the appalling mess I would create. No amount of tidying would ever hide the harsh scars of stumps and the enormous blackened pits of burned brush piles. At Nuk Tessli, from the start, trees were selected with great care as to the aesthetic look of the place and attempts were made to fall them where they would do least damage even to small shrubs and bushes. The stumps were disguised as much as possible by being sliced to the ground and covered with rocks or interesting pieces of wood. Even so, I could not avoid leaving a few of them visible. Burning was rejected as a means of brush disposal for in this high, dry, slow-growing climate, the fire scars would be visible for generations. So limbs and branches were piled as discreetly as possible and for a while they supplied all summer cookwood and kindling. Chainsaw lumber making was another mess-maker for it produced huge quantities of a sawdust so dense it would not brush off the rocks without the application of a scrub-brush and water. If it seemed a little ridiculous to be out there in the bush with a bucket and mop, the rapid blending back to nature was worth it.

For the first three years that I lived here, there were enough building offcuts to keep me in firewood. Most of this lay in a small swamp a few hundred yards north of the cabin and was hauled home on a pack frame or occasionally, in winter, by toboggan. This wood is now history and it has been supplemented with beetle-killed pine, pockets of which are scattered throughout the district. Most of this wood is farther away from home than the building offcuts and it is more practical to bring it in by canoe; however, the last thing I want are stumps that are visible from the water as has happened on all the other inhabited lakes in the area. When I first arrived here, the only sign of man was a few ancient trap blazes above a trail that had long since disappeared at one end of the lake: cabins apart, I want to keep it that way. So the easy trees, the ones that stand next to or lean over the water, are left alone and the selections are made farther back from the shore.

Like berry picking, and in fact most activities at Nuk Tessli, fire-wood gathering is governed by the seasons. Sometimes logging begins during the winter. Much of the waterfront is a thick jumble of rocks and tangled skirts of balsam fir; in summer this presents an insurmountable barrier but deep winter snow covers a lot of the obstacles and facilitates getting the wood to the waterfront. In the fall, suitable targets are marked: trees whose stumps will be hidden by brush but which are otherwise not too contorted or too far from the lake. Snowshoes are not the best footwear for falling trees, but the snow would be prohibitive without them. Preparations have to be made several days in advance; the snow is tramped over daily and well packed down near the trunk and over my escape routes. If I do this on a warm afternoon in late February or March, with luck the snow is hard by morning; if it still won't bear my weight I take the snowshoes off and use them as a platform. Falling trees is one of my least favourite occupations; even after all these years I still approach the chainsaw with dread.

Sixty feet is a tall tree in this climate, but some are as much as two feet thick at the butt. Because of the altitude they are branchy and knotty, full of burls and contortions induced by insects and mistletoe, a far cry from the smooth, easily split rounds encountered by the enthusiastic essay-writer. But it is all I have, and although their knots and warts and close annual rings—the latter often so close together that they cannot be counted—makes for a splitting nightmare, once in the stove, they give off a good supply of heat.

Most of the building offcuts were small enough to be packed home in rounds that could be split at leisure through the winter. But loading heavy objects in and out of a canoe is hard on the back so the wood must all be axed before I can bring it home. I tell myself it would be advisable to do that in the winter as well as the falling, but somehow I never get around to it and keep putting it off; finally, it has to be done and by then it has become a curse.

Hauling the wood by canoe is best done in the late summer or fall because at that time the lake is about four feet lower than in the spring; at high water the most convenient areas for loading the boat are unavailable. An average-sized tree fills a canoe and takes perhaps two hours to split; I need a dozen or so canoe-loads a year. I have become quite adept at stuffing stove-lengths under thwarts and seats and piling them to a monstrous height above the gunwales. I leave a tiny space at the back to sit in, my feet on a log and knees against my chin. I have about an inch of freeboard and the canoe is extremely top-heavy, wobbling at a touch. The boat handles like an oil tanker— sluggish to start, slow to turn and difficult to stop: I always hit the tires that cushion my wharf with more force than I intend. But those few moments on the water are invariably pleasant, for a load like that can be brought in only when the lake is dead calm and at its pristine best.

One year I had an unexpected companion for my wood-hauling activities. He first appeared while a group of hikers, with whom I had been away for a few days, was sitting on my deck waiting for their pick-up plane. A sparrow-sized bird, freckled and ridiculously tame, hopped about among the crumbs on the makeshift table. He had not been around before, and no birds had been fed through the summer, so his instant presumption that we would succour him was a bit of a mystery. The spotted, nondescript coat and the hint of yellow baby lips around the beak marked him for a youngster; I came to the conclusion in the end that he was a fox sparrow who was a little confused about just what species he belonged to.

The hikers duly left and the sparrow adopted me wholeheartedly. The most practical routine for me at that time was to split and bring in a load of wood first thing in the morning, thus taking advantage of the coolness and calm, then work inside away from the black flies. For lunch breaks I grabbed a sandwich and sat on the deck. The bird soon learned to wait for me at the door. He would flutter beside me along the walkway and, although the table might be littered with crumbs, if I did not give him a chunk of bread right away, he would land on my sandwich, feet tromping in the jam, and peck furiously at it, even while the other end was in my mouth.

He followed everything that moved, including the dogs; even a trip to the outhouse was no longer sacrosanct. One morning I went for the usual load of wood and the bird followed the dogs as they ran along the shore. He sat as closely as possible to me while the canoe was being packed, often perching on the bit of wood I was handling. Finally, the boat was full and I cautiously eased myself into the stern. The bird flew at once onto the load and preened himself like Nefertiti on the Nile all the way back to the wharf.

Fox sparrows are beautiful singers and their clear melodies are very much a feature of the sub-alpine spring in these parts. They quit singing around the middle of July when the parents' energies are devoted to raising their young. In the fall they often start up again in a limited way; I suppose it is a kind of call to arms before they begin their migration. (I don't think fox sparrows go far but just move to a

kinder climate.) The day that the first autumn song sounded, my little bird vanished. He must have suddenly remembered he was a fox sparrow after all. Unless, of course, the dogs ate him.

The final stage of the firewood hauling is not in the least dangerous but it is the most tedious and mind-numbing job of all. Hitherto, all my operations have been aided by gravity, for the prime object has been to get the wood down. Now I have to carry it up. Because of knee problems I can manage only two or three stove-lengths at a time. It must require three or four miles of tramping back and forth per canoe-load for this operation. Up three rock steps, up four wooden ones, along the deck past the bored and dozing dogs who have nothing to do but lie in the sun and wait to be taken for their walk, and up the final small slope into the woodshed. On the rocky and uneven ground there were few sites available for this building. I can see absolutely no way of getting out of this chore save abusing the shoreline or constructing a floating shed and anchoring it to the wharf which, even if it would survive the winds and the ice, would, as far as I am concerned, be aesthetically unacceptable.

*Chris Czajkowski*

The cleanup of my logging operations I leave until last—if time or the weather is importunate, that can always be done the following spring. The stumps, especially those which were winter-logged, still contain a round or two of wood, and they are trimmed below brush level. Chips are picked up for kindling and the loose bark and sawdust is swept into the bushes.

For several years I had no help with the firewood, but latterly I have been fortunate enough to find a few young bucks who enjoy flexing their muscles in return for some wilderness experience. I am a tall, strong woman, but I can never compete with a man for muscle power. When I think of the long, slow hours I have struggled with physical tasks since I have been here, I marvel at the male physique and am envious of a man's casual indifference to his strength.

The nine-to-five, five-day-a-week schedule and its attendant calendar of commercial extravaganzas have been designed for an artificial world where climate is no longer an issue. Outside the parameters of city walls, such measurements become meaningless. I try (not always successfully) to keep track of the date in order to coordinate with the outside world when I feel it is necessary, but I do not own a clock. I design my activities around the wind, the weather and the seasons. I take great pleasure in the flowerings and the ripenings of the plants and the migrations of the animals, but my relationship with them runs deeper, for I am also bound by their routines. I must put aside all other work when the berries are ripe for they will not wait. I canoe up the lake in the morning so that I will not have to fight the wind. The firewood must be packed home before winter or I will be faced with a hellish struggle through soft, deep snow.

Knowing the rhythms of the land makes one look forward to them; participating in them becomes a pilgrimage. Cranberry-picking time is the only occasion when it is practical to walk along the creek bottom—in summer the water roars and a hiker must stick to the trail; in winter the snow bows the alders and forms a bridge and I snowshoe several feet above the water, the creek all but silent, except for a few hollow gurgles far below.

## chapter 7

# zen and the art of being pessimistic

*In cases of emergency, it is folly to hold one's hand and sit down to bewail in abject terror: it is better to be up and doing.*

Catherine Parr Traill, *The Canadian Settler's Guide*

As a writer I am far from the league of those who can claim to support themselves by their art; the tourist business moves slowly—in this day of instant communication people are baffled by my lack of a phone—and after eight years as a treeplanter, pounding trees into cutblocks, my body is beginning to wear out and I prefer to save what is left of it for my own mountains. Even if I needed nothing else, I would still have to find cash to pay for food and its transportation, as well as the land fees the government requires. I would not be content, however, without a great deal more from life than mere sustenance. So lately, in an effort to make money, I have concentrated more on artwork and, with linocut prints of alpine plants as the focus, have started to attend a craft-fair circuit in the fall. With craft fairs every weekend, I cannot possibly come home in between, so while I am on the road I shop, visit, organise business, give art courses and present slide shows to publicise both the tourist business and my books. This means that, once I leave the cabin in the fall, I must plan on being away from it for at least a couple of months.

The first fair, in Prince George, takes place at the beginning of November and, giving myself time for the hike to the road, the drive to Prince George, and the necessary several days' preparation (I do all the matting and plastic-wrapping of the prints and cards at Nimpo) means that cranberry picking marks the end of my year at Nuk Tessli. The craft fair circuit lasts five or six weeks, and as early winter hikes have given me a few bad weather scares, I do not usually return home until the ice is good. Whatever calendar date that may be—sometimes as early as the middle of December and at others as late as the New Year—in practical terms it means a complete change of pace. By the time I get back Nuk Tessli may be buried under four feet of drifted snow or be subject to temperatures of forty below.


I fit the artwork in when I can throughout the year but, what with maintenance of both buildings and trails, visitors, and plant exploration, there is little time in the summer to be creative. If any artwork is ready, it is freighted out on whatever aircraft happens to be going to Nimpo, but if such transport fails to materialize I must charter my own flight at the end of the year. I cannot leave it too late, for the pilots take their aircraft out of the water as soon as ice begins to form on some of the smaller lakes, and in any case, once Thanksgiving is over, there is very little business for them and they are anxious to be away on their well-deserved fall vacations. So I must plan the final flight for the middle of October and I never fail to be in a dither wondering whether or not I have thought of everything that will be needed for the next three months.

If there was only artwork to go out I would simply carry it myself rolled up in an (unused!) length of stove- or sewage-pipe and wrapped in several layers of plastic. It makes for a top-heavy backpack for the package will not fit inside either mine or the dogs' bags, but many an original work has travelled in this way.

There always seems to be a plethora of other bits and pieces to ferry back and forth. Two places of residence, especially as one is so far from a road, complicates the issue; whatever document I might need is inevitably in the wrong place and might be unreachable for

several weeks. So I try and imagine what the land office might desire over the next quarter year (for the conditions under which I am granted this lease are remarkably elastic and there are always new bureaucratic inventions with which to deal); or which manuscripts might suddenly be demanded by a publisher (although this is usually more wishful thinking than anything). As well, the outgoing freight will inevitably include a stack of mail for Lora to take over to the post office for me. A year's accumulation of recyclables—glass and cans—have to be packed up to go; these normally fill only one or two small cartons a year, but they still have to be disposed of. Although Williams Lake has a poor recycling record, other towns on the craft-fair circuit have facilities, so these boxes are lugged about until the opportunity to deal with them arises. If the berry season has been productive, there might be a case of canned wild fruit: my friends are generous with their own produce or locally available luxuries when they come to see me; all I can offer in return is a small taste of the high-altitude wild. Most of my town clothes are stored at Nimpo but it could be forty below before I come back, so extra socks, sweaters and a second sleeping bag are stuffed into containers. A carton of borrowed books is made ready to return to their owners; as is an empty kerosene can to be filled in Williams Lake where it is sold in bulk and therefore at a much cheaper rate; and perhaps a chunk of hollow log for a friend to use as a planter. In like manner, good burls split from firewood rounds will be flown out for another friend who is a carver.

One of the problems at this time of year is not knowing exactly when, or how, I will be able to get home again. Items like toboggans, snowshoes and a trail axe must be outside in case I travel back on foot, so if they are not already at Nimpo, they must be sent on the plane. The cabin, too, needs to be organised. There is no plumbing to worry about, nor water-cooled engines to drain or spike with anti-freeze (except my truck, but that will be attended to outside), but there are a multitude of jobs that must be done.

The root cellar always needs attention; mice have tunnelled and nested in the two-foot-thick fibreglass wall insulation and their holes must be blocked. They will make more, but at least the cellar will start the winter with a solid barrier of warmth. All the food in the garbage cans in the attic must be examined in order to make a detailed shopping list for I will be in towns with stores and, with luck, I will have money to spend. The canoes must be dragged from the wharf and propped vertically against trees so that they won't be crushed by heavy snow. A good stack of kindling and small wood must be split; a load of wood has to be stuffed into the second cabin. (I keep emergency supplies in it all winter in case my own house burns down.) I need to remove the fly screens and seal the windows; give the chimney a last sweep and take down the roof ladder to give the snow the maximum chance to slide freely; and finally do all the things I always do when I leave: pack breakables and food (except freezeables; they will have to take their chances in the root cellar) up the ladder into the (hopefully) bear-proof attic; put up the shutters; fill the lamps and store them where the squirrels can't knock them over if they get into the house; dismantle the photovoltaic system so that it won't short out and cause a fire if something bites through the wires—after making sure the batteries are fully charged to ensure that they will not freeze; place the solar panels by a certain tree (they are on a long cord and moveable) so that I shall be sure of being able to find them beneath the snow; put matches in jars so they cannot be ignited by little chewing teeth; upend all buckets to stop mice committing suicide in them (which they puzzlingly but invariably do, whether the buckets are empty or not); lay a fire ready in the big, barrel heater; and wire the door shut as I leave. It is amazing how wind and animals can work at a door in the wilderness.

Although the plane picks up the freight, I prefer to travel overland. Firstly, the dogs and I take up more than half the space within a plane and with a big load of freight this would necessitate paying for another flight. But the journey has a deeper purpose for it reaffirms my place within the country and eases the transition between the wilderness and the outside world. Besides, my truck is still parked at the ranch, halfway to Nimpo, and I do not want the bother of either walking fifteen miles back on the logging road—not the same thing at all as hiking in the bush—or begging a lift from a friend, to retrieve it.

Pessimism is an integral part of a wilderness-dweller's make-up; unless you can imagine everything that might possibly go wrong, you cannot be prepared for it when it does. What if a late bear breaks in and not only opens the way for the snow to drift into the cabin, but also wrecks the root cellar and spoils my reserve of food? (The shotgun trap would not be left at this point; when snow dumps off the roof it can shake the cabin and I have no desire to find that it has discharged the gun and achieved the same result as the bear. If Gold Tip decides to enter it cannot be helped—all the books below the window have been moved aside just in case—but so far there have been no bears about at this time of year; presumably they are all farther west down on the Atnarko River, feasting on the spawning salmon. Many of them will, however, climb back into the alpine to den.) Is the roof strong enough to withstand an unprecedented snow dump without me being there to shovel it? Could there be a lightning strike? (Don't laugh at that one: several trees have been hit in the area; one only yards from the cabin was struck during the storm I witnessed from the lookout.) But as one foot follows the other, measuring the miles to the outside world, one thought will override every other worry: "What have I forgotten?"

# chapter 8

# humpty dumpty must have been a logger

*"When I use a word," Humpty Dumpty said in a rather scorn-
ful tone, "It means just what I choose it to mean—neither more
nor less."*

*"The question is," said Alice, "whether you can make words
mean so many different things."*

*"The question is," said Humpty Dumpty," "which is to be mas-
ter—that's all."*

Lewis Carroll, *Alice Through the Looking Glass*

I have sometimes been asked what I will do when I am sixty-five (as
if retirement from wilderness-dwelling is mandatory at that age).
While compromises will undoubtedly have to be made, my usual reply is: "By that time there will be a road running past my door." This
comment has produced laughter, but it is not really meant as a joke.

When I came to Canada, I chose British Columbia because of the
mountains; I also figured that such a large province housing only
three million people, most of whom lived in a comparatively small
area, must have a lot of untouched country left. But even when I
arrived twenty years ago, I was astounded to see the mark so few

people had made on such a large territory. The accelerated speed with which the wilderness has since been destroyed is frightening.

At present my "backyard" is protected on three sides by water. Charlotte Lake and the main branch of the Atnarko lie to the north; the McLinchy guards the south; and the great four-thousand-foot-deep trough in Tweedsmuir Provincial Park forms a pretty effective barrier to the west. Recently, two breaches over these natural fences have been proposed. One is a bridge across the Atnarko close to where it leaves Charlotte Lake, to permit the development of a small business logging contract to salvage blow down, and the other is a gold mine on the mountain which sits halfway between my cabin and the ranch where my truck is stored. At the moment, these proposals appear remote both in distance and time; mere mosquito bites upon the placid surface of my existence. But, if they eventuate, it will mean the end of this area as it now exists.

Like Humpty Dumpty in Alice's looking glass, the logging industry is a master of obfuscating English. Words do not always say what, in other circumstances, they usually mean. Take the word "forest" itself. It is used to describe any group of trees, be it diverse in age and content as is created by nature, or thousands of acres of sterile, monoculture plantation no more than six feet high; the latter has about the same relationship to a natural forest as does a golf course to the Amazon jungle. "Over mature" and "decadent" are deliberately debilitating terms the industry has coined to denigrate old growth. "Selective logging" refers to several different procedures, most of which are nowhere near as kind as the general public would like to believe. Whereas community woodlots can be carefully harvested to produce more standing timber at the end of a human generation than there was at the beginning, supporting both the operators and nature's bio-diversity requirements in the meantime, the industry's "selective logging" definitions range from: taking all conifers and leaving only deciduous trees, and cutting down everything marketable and leaving diseased and weak specimens that will never be of commercial use; to taking a few trees out of a stand, thus encouraging the remainder to put on size, then, twenty years later, cutting down the rest. More board feet per hectare might have been achieved within those twenty years, but the biological result is still a clearcut and (if it grows to schedule) an absolute minimum of three human generations on the coast and six in the interior will have to pass before the plantation will produce any more income.

Let us look at a "salvage" contract for the small business program. Salvage is a very useful word for the logging industry. Firstly, the very term denotes a moral excellence in making use of "waste" despite the fact that dead trees have long been proven to be very necessary in a multitude of ways for a healthy ecosystem: long-term plantations in Europe are sickening from this very lack, and New Zealanders are deliberately dynamiting trees to provide dead and decaying snags. Single-age plantations cannot support hole-dwelling birds and small animals who eat harmful insects and transport seeds and spores, essential services for the health of a forest. Secondly, salvage contracts take out all the trees in a cutblock, not just the dead ones; in many cases the injured specimens are very much the smaller proportion of the total logged (thirty percent of affected trees is all that is legally required for a beetle-kill block). Thirdly, and this is far more serious, all salvage contracts, no matter how large, are not included in the basic Annual Allowable Cut. For the Williams Lake area alone, 2.46 million cubic feet are slated for the Annual Allowable Cut. Salvage and beetle-kill blocks bring that figure to 3.8 million cubic feet, a third as much again. According to the 1997 report *Overcutting the Chilcotin*, these mills in Williams Lake are in fact "currently logging fifty-four percent more trees each year than the provincial government estimates is sustainable." One Williams Lake mill alone requires the contents of ninety logging trucks a day to function. This town needs fourteen hundred cubic meters of timber logged to sustain one job: the rest of Canada maintains two jobs per one thousand cubic metres and in New Zealand five people are employed for the same amount.

The small blow-down contract north of my cabin along the

Atnarko, taken in isolation, might not be very harmful to the environment. After all, trees have to come from somewhere and contractors do need work. But the road would cross the principal tributary of the third-largest Pacific salmon spawning ground in B.C. and, to conform to the Forest Practices Code, it would have to be "back-hauled" (i.e., each load of rock and gravel would have to be trucked to a less sensitive place and dumped, rather than merely pushed over the bank) to avoid massive erosion and silting of the river. This is a very expensive way to build a road and because it would service the small business program, it would be government funded. Such largess would not, of course, be used for one project only but would open the way for all sorts of development.

What is worse, the term "small business program" has connotations that are far from understood by the majority. It sounds wonderful: here is the small company bucking the big guys. But an area designated for the small business program enfolds a number of operators and may be quite big in extent. A timber volume is guaranteed and, because many environmental practices are expensive, ecological restrictions may be waived, making it overall the most destructive kind of logging tenure. A good example is the horribly abused country in the reservoir area north of Revelstoke, where I tree-planted for a season; the results of industrial activity, I am afraid, make big companies like Macmillan-Bloedel look like environmental gurus in comparison.

But none of the logging would really matter very much if it wasn't for the roads. Roads and wilderness simply cannot co-exist. John Perlin, in *A Forest Journey* (New York, 1989), provides an excellent selection of historical records showing man's relationship to and subsequent destruction of his forests. Wood was, until recently, the only source of fuel for many industrial operations: making eating utensils, glass and the engines of war, as well as for building and cooking. But although communities suffered hardships and had to move on, and Greek and Roman harbours silted up due to clearcutting along the rivers (despite dire warnings about their logging practices from contemporary writers), logs could not be transported very far on land. The rape of the forests was confined to a narrow margin by the edge of a stretch of water, either fresh or salt, that was big enough to float a log; this still left a lot of country which could not be violated.

Once canals and wheeled vehicles that could handle heavy loads were built, the ecology of an area often fell apart. When massive cutblocks appeared recently north of Charlotte Lake (for "beetle-kill harvest"), people came from all over Western Canada to enjoy the boom in hunting. Logging companies always claim an increase in the number of animals shot on cutblocks is due to a resurgence of their feed which appears once the tree cover is removed, and this well may be the case in some instances. But the industry is still determined to treat the dry, high, short-season Interior as if it were the year-round, wet climate of the coast. (It makes one wonder what industry biologists are taught.) North of Charlotte Lake, it was not browse that increased the kill—even after a dozen years there is little plant life much taller than a dandelion and still a great deal of barren, machine-churned ground on these blocks—the hunting figures were boosted solely by the increased visibility of the game and the roads which allowed vehicular access. Five years after the first road went in, moose became so scarce they were put on a draw for the first time ever.

Most of the rest of the Chilcotin still bears sparse, dry forest, but already the greater part of it has been bid for, and it will soon succumb to the feller chainsaw bunchers. Ten years ago this type of forest was garbage. But now loggers have to turn to the Chilcotin as other areas are rapidly being desecrated. New automated processes mean that mills are hungrier than ever (even though they are laying off workers) and there is nowhere else left to go. Despite some restrictions to the industry via the recent Forest Practices Code, the province-wide Annual Allowable Cut has not been reduced, and "salvage" contracts continue to be assigned in excess of it. The speed with which the forests are being destroyed has in no way been halted or even slowed. Residents of more populated areas might rejoice that their own forest remnants have some hope, but the industrial "harvest" is now being concentrated in hitherto ignored districts, whose timber volume is so paltry that huge areas must be flattened to keep pouring the trees into the mills. Industry is designing a future based on building materials made from "safe" chemicals and chips, and for that any species or quality of tree will do. At these higher elevations, tree-shaded ground causes snow to lie for weeks after that on bare land has gone, and cutting huge areas will cause early runoff and therefore a serious spring flooding and a shortage of water in summer for even far-flung parts of the province. Additionally a fluctuation of river levels may seriously impede the ability of spawning salmon to find their way to their breeding grounds. None of these facts have so far filtered through the thick heads of decision-makers. There are none so blind as those who do not wish to see.

On a smaller scale, private property is also affected by industrial development. Here in the "wild west" (as residents of Williams Lake refer to the Chilcotin) we attract a good number of the more destructive kind of recreationist who is never without a rifle and who shoots everything that moves and several things that don't. The residents who are beginning to settle on the north shore of Charlotte Lake have had windows shot out and boats holed or removed. The people who indulge in these activities, moreover, do not stick to roads. The forest highways are now so close to the alpine that it takes little work for recreationists to cut their own routes through sparse timber to the tree line and drive where they please over the wide alpine plateaus which are such a dominant feature of the eastern edge of the central Coast Range. ATVs and snowmachines used indiscriminately can rapidly reduce swamps to mudpiles and fragile soils to mulch. The perpetrators are often by no means deliberate in their destruction. Their city-oriented education has made no effort to put them in touch with the workings of the environment and they cannot imagine that the endless "barren" rock and duff and exciting mudholes which they revel in "conquering" might be in any way ecologically important.


I challenge anyone, even the most learned biologist, to give me an iron-clad formula which quantifies environmental sustainablility. Government publications have the gall to claim that they now understand it, but that is nonsense. The more anyone learns about an ecosystem, the more complicated and the more impossible to control he realises that it is. Management of the wilderness is simply a euphemism for managing the short-term cash flow. The majority of decision-makers have always lived in cities and they always will. City folk have always imagined themselves to be sophisticated and worldly, but step back and look at these artificial microcosms, and each one is revealed to be

*Chris Czajkowski*

as insular and parochial as any society on earth. Their inhabitants quote the artifices and dogma of their masters. Humpty Dumpty was right. "When I use a word it means just what I choose it to mean." As long as he was master, that is.

And we all know what happened to Humpty Dumpty in the end.

## chapter 9

# *saxifraga saga*

*He was a botanist. Used to collect all sorts of silly little wildflowers, the kind you wouldn't look at twice.*

Agatha Christie, *By the Pricking of My Thumbs*

The mountain on which the gold mining claim sits is directly on my summer route to the road; I therefore cross one part or another of it several times in a year. It is right on the border between the volcanic plateau of the Chilcotin and the upthrust fold mountains of the granite Coast Range, and it contains a mixture of both soil types. It has proved to be my best hunting ground for plants and hosts several species not found elsewhere in the area, no doubt because of the different minerals that are present.

As a botanist and tree-planter, I know much more about forests than I do about the mining industry. Geologists have looked at the area before and found little to interest them so one hopes there is no great quantity of gold sitting on the mountain. However, modern extraction methods and soaring gold prices might make the difference. The claims were staked by flying in by helicopter—an expensive machine to use—but a road to that site, which is above the tree line, would be long and tortuous; it would also be very costly, both for the industry as well as the environment. I don't know if chemicals would be used during the extraction process but they would be another concern and might well affect a nearby high-altitude fly-in fishing lake, one much used by local resorts, and so far the highest earner of tourist dollars in the area.

This mountain is ten miles from my cabin; I see it from my eastern window and watch the sun rise over it in August and April. The claim is on an odd red streak of rock, most certainly volcanic in origin, which splits the mountain and forms a saddle on top and gullies on both sides. The north-facing cut, down which runs a creek permanently fed by a large snow patch near the summit, contains at least one species of plant which, because of its absence from most of my large collection of field guides, would appear to be uncommon at the least. The plant is *Saxifraga adscendens* —I don't think it has a popular name.

Ten miles is a huge distance to a city-dweller. You who live within sight, sound or on top of other people might complain about your neighbours but cannot imagine an existence without them. Even if you go into the wilderness you congregate at resorts or travel about in large groups. (Compare yourselves with eider ducks. These birds normally nest within noisy seabird colonies, seeking safety in their host's numbers. People who wish to encourage the ducks to handier sites, so that they can more easily collect the down from their nests, must erect flags and pinwheels and other inanimate agitators and noise makers to make the ducks feel comfortable.)

City-dwellers are not only baffled by a desire to live like I do, many also feel that it is not right, that I am selfish to demand conditions over such a large tract of land. When someone first accused me of this I was enormously surprised. Wasn't everyone aware of the need for huge untouched areas, particularly in the fringe climates of mountains and deserts, to maintain a cohesive and viable environment? Apparently not. It certainly had not occurred to me that an unspoiled wilderness was not desired by others. But upon reflection, I have to concede that there is a strong streak of selfishness to my creed. There have always been those of us who need space in a way that the city-dweller cannot fathom—after all, it was people like me who, for better or worse, originally opened up the country that urban residents now inhabit with ease. I have spent an enormous amount of time and effort to create the kind of life I want and I do not wish to see it destroyed—and destroyed, moreover, not because someone's livelihood is at stake, but simply because a select group wants to drink more beer or possess a new ATV.

If my attitudes are uncharitable, is the demand of city amenities as a *right*, not equally self-indulgent? I am talking about paved roads, limitless electric power, clean water, garbage disposal. These are luxuries. The majority of the world's peoples exist without them. But the presence of these amenities are so habitual in most western peoples' existence that they are taken for granted. They think that all they have to do is hand over a few dollars and everything will be provided. But what it really means is that the environment they abuse is out of sight and out of mind, and in somebody else's backyard.

It is no good saying there is no room for my attitudes any more, there is also no room for unthinking resource extraction. I cannot fight genetics or whatever it is that has made me what I am. And if I was not here, who would plead the case for *Saxifraga adscendens*? Who would even know it was here?

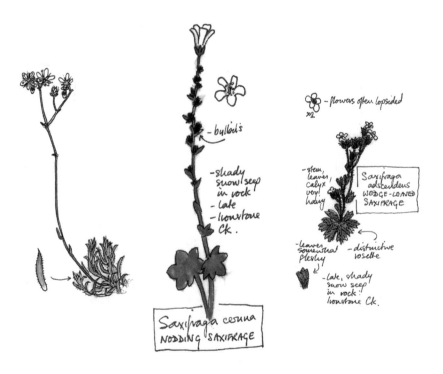

Saxifraga cernua
NODDING SAXIFRAGE

Further exploration of the red-rock creek has taken me into the centre of the claim itself. A corner post has been planted on a knoll, and blue flagging tape tied to rocks on the far side of the creek marks the other extremities. The rectangle they delineate encloses a mini-canyon along a short section of the creek bed that is topped on one side by a cornice. The shady seepage of water that trickles continuously from it has nurtured an amazing Saxifrage garden. Along with a few more specimens of *Saxifraga adscendens,* no less than eight other species within that genus grace this spot, including an unusual population of a white form of *Saxifraga oppositifolia,* which, even in its purple phase, is quite rare in this area, although the latter is common in the Rockies and the Arctic. White-flowered and purple-flowered plants bloom side by side in this spot, and that must make the location unique.

Each of the couple of dozen specimens of *Saxifraga adscendens* boasts no more than two inches of height and sports a tiny cluster of white blossoms at its apex. They hug the shade and lie in crannies, hidden from all but the most observant eye. This "silly little plant that no one else would look twice at" is not as environmentally marketable as a grizzly bear, nor does it have the charisma of a raft-run river. It is not, therefore, the sort of thing that is likely to mobilize busloads of linked-armed demonstrators to sing, pray and give obeisance to the god of environmentalism. Nor can I offer an economic argument for protection of the plant. Even if it contained the wonder-drug of the century, no one is ever going to believe that a pocket of two dozen specimens could possible compete with the proven authority of gold.

This country is very sparsely populated and cries against industrial development will therefore be few. Some residents will indeed welcome such invasions with dreams of more cash or a bigger selection of roads down which to manipulate the new recreation vehicles they have bought with their timber dollars.

I have dutifully sent letters to various ministries and received arms-embossed envelopes containing thank yous for my concerns and assurances that everyone is considering the matter most conscientiously, and that the sustainability of the environment is of the highest priority. With poor radio reception, no television, and without phone, fax, newspapers or computer mail, however, it is difficult for me to keep abreast of politics, a subject for which I have very little affinity anyway. Luckily, the defense of the Charlotte Alplands (some bureaucrat must have termed that one—it is not a local name) is in much more capable hands than mine. Dan and Kathy Ressl coordinate the residents on the north shore of Charlotte Lake. Frank Naumann and his wife Paulina run a summer fishing resort on a fly-in lake very close to where the logging bridge is proposed (about fifteen miles from me as the crow flies, but as the mountains are too abrupt between us to make the journey directly, it would take two days to reach it). Frank has an impressive ability to formulate graphs and other documentary data in the same language that an employee of the government would use. And forty miles northwest of my cabin live the nearest neighbours in that direction, Dave and Rosemary Neads. Dave is a full-blooded politician and he revels in it; his wife is a perfect partner to his aspirations. Environmental lobbyists are usually city dwellers; many have little actual understanding of the wilderness; very few people of Dave and Rosemary's beliefs and talents choose to live so thoroughly on the job.

One year, I spent Christmas at Dave and Rosemary's place. Before that, we had exchanged notes through the post office, spoken to each other on the phone and even bumped into each other once in a while when we both happened to be collecting mail at the same time. But wilderness friendships are never formal. We know all that is necessary about each other long before we meet; no matter how diverse our backgrounds, we have something in common which automatically binds us together. It is our desire to be here. This choice which so many outside people seem to find puzzling, and which is very difficult to quantify in city language, needs no explanation amongst ourselves. We will no doubt find each other strongly individualistic, a quality that is inseparable from the lifestyle, but to each other we will never be incomprehensible.

Dave and Rosemary live at The Precipice. I had heard quite a bit about this valley from one of the other two families that own property there, but I had never been there and was curious to see it. The Precipice is an anomaly in this part of the world. Everywhere else in the area, when the red, volcanic Chilcotin plateau meets the uncompromising granite of the Coast Range, the result is rocks and bluffs and dizzying drops fit only for birds and goats. But The Precipice

Valley, big enough for a couple of ranches, is a complete world on its own that hangs halfway between the two ecosystems. It is lower and has more moderate temperatures than the Chilcotin but has only half the rainfall of the Coast. Or, to put it in gardening terms, tomatoes can be grown, but they must be ripened under glass.

The game of politics is as baffling to me as the workings of the wilderness are to most city folk. Dave, however, terming himself a grass roots conservationist, thrives on it. Despite the inaccessible place in which he lives, he is prepared to spend the year not only travelling to meetings all over the province, but also enduring, even enjoying, what seems to me (at the few meetings I have attended) to be the most tortuous, time-consuming, money-wasting pettiness. Admittedly, I have not been present at enough of the meetings to understand the rules. Politician-speak might as well be a dialect from Mars as far as I am concerned. For instance, at a Land Resource Use Plan meeting in Williams Lake, where about forty representatives of different land users—environmental groups, tourism operators, logging companies and trades unions—took the whole day, the evening included, to try and reach a consensus on the meaning of "consensus." I've no doubt that all these machinations are comprehensible to some, and might even be essential, but if that is democracy, I can do nothing but sit helplessly in the wings while my fate is decided.


The direct route to The Precipice from my cabin would take me across three trackless mountains; not an impossible feat but a difficult one that I certainly would not want to tackle in the middle of winter. A more plausible route on foot would involve picking up a game trail I once found leading down into Tweedsmuir Park, the only breach in the precipitous walls for miles, then hike for two days along the Atnarko River past my old cabin near Lonesome Lake and strike up a steep path known as the Sugar Camp Trail. This journey might be fun to do sometime, but it would still be a formidable undertaking in December. The easiest way to reach The Precipice from Nuk Tessli is to go out to Nimpo, go north along the highway to Anahim, then back in along the Neads' twenty-mile road, which is snowmachine-only in winter. As I am not enough of a mechanic to want to risk owning one of these contraptions myself (it would break down two days' walk from anywhere and then where would I be?) Dave came out to fetch me. I could have ridden in relative comfort on the padded seat behind him if I did not have Lonesome. She was not getting any younger and she would not be able to run behind. She would have to ride in the skimmer towed behind the snowmachine and, because she would not stay in it alone, I would have to sit in there with her.

I have travelled this way before and it is not the most pleasant method of covering ground. But the alternative was to snowshoe in and, whereas a foot trail might have offered some enjoyment, lifting one foot in front of the other on a road is simply tedious. In the skimmer I was flung about with abandon; a gas can leaked all over both myself and the dog; it was cold and bone-jarringly bumpy and, despite the baffle on the front of the sled, a solid stream of snow was flung into my face. It is probably no worse in these respects than travelling behind a dog team—judging by Sport, my other dog, who ran easily behind, the speed must be much the same. But dog sled riders would not have to put up with the noise, and the exhaust fumes they would experience would be of a somewhat different nature.

For well over an hour there was no appreciable gain or loss in altitude. We were shut in by the sparse lodgepole pines of the Chilcotin; I kept my eyes glued to what I could see of the trail so I would be ready to duck the occasional snow-laden branch or whipping willow twigs. Then the snow grew deeper, the vegetation turned to spruce and suddenly we ran against a log fence with glimpses of a lot of nothing beyond. Dave stopped and switched off the motor. The dog leapt gratefully out and I heaved myself to my feet, fingers and toes tingling from the vibration. We were perched on top of the abrupt conclusion of the Chilcotin's sheet of ancient volcanic magma. Beneath our feet was the organ-pipe wall of basalt that gives The Precipice its name. Far below was a calm, white sweep of meadow dotted with three groups of doll-like buildings, each accompanied by a blue feather of smoke. They were linked by meandering cow trails and the green, ice-choked skeins of the Precipice River. We were standing in sunshine, instantly warm after the tree-shadowed, tumultuous ride. Melting ice tinkled off the big Douglas firs that graced the steep slopes of the valley, the sound blending with the murmur of the distant river. It looked gentle, quite a contrast to either the raw Chilcotin or the rugged coastal country below.

There are currently two full-time and two part-time families living in the valley. Dave and Rosemary have the only new dwelling; they built it themselves with hand-sawn trees horse-logged from their property. They moved into the new house four years ago although, as with most such endeavours, it was far from finished.

The main living area is well-designed both for comfort and to accommodate the wonderful view. Because they can drive on a road in summer (albeit a rough one) their possessions, unlike mine, are not restricted to those which fit into a plane. And because they have sixteen solar panels (compared with my two) and a generator backup, they can run as many electrical tools and gadgets as they want. They have a computer (of course) and lights—even lights on the Christmas tree. The latter were perhaps symbols of their achievements for, judging by the proprietorial pride with which they enjoyed them (and the small ration of time that they were lit), they most certainly were not taken for granted.

But a piece of technology that is a real peculiarity of the place, and one to which very few wilderness dwellers can aspire, is a phone. Not a radiophone, but a land phone: a telephone. Connected by a twenty-mile phone line to Anahim Lake.

We had come in under that line, dodging back and forth beneath the poles. It follows what was once the main communication route between the Chilcotin plateau and the coast. Despite the ruggedness of the country, several of these routes were already well established by the natives before European settlers entered the picture. Black volcanic glass, ideal for tool-making, was traded down from the Interior, and dried salmon and oolichan oil was packed up. The latter has given the name "grease trails" to these routes. Settlers quickly made the Precipice passage into a horse trail and it was once even touted for a railroad. But a severe bluff created a problem and, in the fifties, when an automobile road was initiated, politics embraced the present collection of switchbacks known as The Hill. Recent requests by logging companies to bulldoze a way through The Precipice have so far been held at bay by both Fisheries (the river at the bottom being a prime spawning bed) and the managers of Tweedsmuir Provincial Park who are trying to preserve one of the few remaining active grizzly habitats in the world.

The settlers' culture required a far different technology from that which revolved around obsidian and oolichan grease. Between 1914 and 1916 a telegraph line was erected. With the fear of a Japanese invasion after Pearl Harbour, the line was upgraded to voice. In the meantime, because someone has always lived at The Precipice and paid the bills, the phone has been kept viable. This is invaluable to Dave and Rosemary, for with it they can make use of modems, fax machines and electronic mail. And with these tools and their expertise, the preservation of the Charlotte Alplands has an element of hope.

Since I discovered *Saxifraga adscendens*, I have learned that it is not as rare as I had first supposed. I have come upon it in The Rainbows, a classic group of volcanoes farther north, and Porsild's *Rocky Mountain Wildflowers* describes it as "occasional to common by alpine brooks and in wet rock crevices" for that range.

But that is not really the point. It is possible that the mining claim will prove to be not economically viable and I sincerely hope that that is the case. And before any test drillings are done. The creek might be sacrificed without a great deal of ecological impact (although I personally would be devastated to see that wonderful Saxifrage garden go). But, as with so many other ecosystems that have already succumbed, the road that would open up the mine for development would signal the end of the wilderness.

*Chris Czajkowski*

# chapter 10

## *flight*

*Oh I have slipped the surly bonds of earth*
*And danced the skies on laughter-silvered wings ...*

John Gillespie Magee, Jr., *High Flight*

It is New Year's Eve. The inhabitants of Nimpo and Anahim Lakes will be gathering to celebrate in the usual way; there's even a band coming all the way from Kamloops to play in the hall. But two days ago, there were signs that the long, calm spell of Christmas weather was coming to an end. The wind had switched to the west and the temperature had risen, and thin layers of cloud were beginning to infiltrate from the coast. It often happens that way: Christmas week will be cold and calm then right around New Year there will be a dump of snow. I had fun with friends over Christmas but did not want to get stranded at Nimpo any longer than could be helped, so last night, with the indications that a coastal front was on its way, I gave Avnorth a call and arranged for Floyd to take me home this morning.

Fresh snow and flying do not mix. It is not just the reduced visibility when the white stuff falls that creates problems, but also the legacy it leaves on the lakes. A heavy dump will push down the ice and cause water to well up through the cracks. Even in very cold temperatures, the snow cover insulates the water and prevents it from freezing so that it remains sandwiched between the snow and the solid ice below. If the skis of a plane break through into this over-flow, the aircraft may have great difficulty in taking off. If the air is cold, the sludge freezes instantly to the skis, rendering them useless, and chopping them free can be a major problem. But warm tempera-tures can be nearly as bad. One time, when it was five above and the foot-deep covering of snow on the ice had the consistency of cooked porridge, Floyd had to taxi the plane up and down the lake half a dozen times to make a runway before he could get up enough speed to break free.

There is a formidable amount of freight to go in with me. The craft-fair circuit has taken me to cities and stores and, while others were fighting the Christmas crowds, I frequented the warehouses and less popular departments for the bulk of my annual shopping. Aside from art supplies such as a heavy order of print-making paper, I had a whole range of other necessities—a couple of cartons of books; bulk hiking food and seeds and grains for bread; a spare pack frame and a pair of boots; two thirty-pound buckets of honey; six forty-five-pound bags of dog food; twenty-two pounds of oats and the same of organic, brown rice; three forty-five-pound bags of whole-wheat flour; twenty-two pounds of wheat berries for grinding; a case of canned tomatoes, a second of green beans and a third of mush-rooms; about fifty tins of sardines (which is how many there are in a case); and, because I am unable to grow much more than radishes up here, about a hundred and fifty pounds of potatoes; a sack of onions; boxes of carrots, cabbages, turnips and parsnips; a few yams and sweet potatoes; a case of apples and bags of oranges; garlic bulbs and ginger roots; seeds for sprouting; half a small steer cut into five large chunks; a miscellany of herbs and spices; income tax forms; an economy pack of toilet paper and the same of detergent; camera film, stamps, enve-lopes, pens; a gas can full of kerosene; the little chainsaw (which I had been using outside); six large boxes of matches; salt; five pounds of butter and a case of lard; six dozen of Mary's eggs; plus a box of bits and pieces, mostly odd clothes, paperwork and Christmas good-ies. Then there are snowshoes, the toboggan and other bulky winter hiking equipment, my two dogs, and lastly, myself. All of this fills my pickup and is far too much for one flight; the two dogs and myself take up more than half a load alone.

I have an irrational dread of flying. Which is a shame, for the world is fascinating from a single-engine plane. My apprehension is increased by the Pacific front which has greyed the sky by sunrise, for it means the air will be turbulent and bumpy. "It's just like getting into a car," I tell myself each time I strap myself beside the pilot. "And it's less than half an hour." The motor fires and the noise is at once deafening. Forward vision is veiled by the blur of the propeller. The aircraft seems light and insubstantial as we move onto the runway. In summer, Floyd takes off from the water in front of his house but in winter he keeps the plane in a heated hangar at the Anahim Lake airport and leaves from there. He takes off on wheels; once in the air, a lever pumps skids under the landing gear.

The country around Anahim is comparatively flat. The scrubby, dark forest, laced with huge, white rectangular cutblocks and the thin connecting threads of logging roads, has the sullen blue-grey cast indicative of snow. The sky is white, the nearer mountains only slightly whiter and the further ones are swallowed by the loom of the storm.

The first ridge appears just before the halfway mark and always creates a small bump of turbulence. That is when I usually close my eyes. But I have travelled the route often enough on foot and can visualise it well: just past the ridge is Charlotte Lake, twelve miles long and five miles wide, the biggest body of water in the area and always the last to freeze. It is sometimes crossable at this time of year but it has been a mild winter so far and the surface looks cracked and greyish and unsafe. Often the whole lake is smothered in a solid, woolly blanket of fog whose abrupt edge exactly follows the contours of the shore; the inhabitants are then shrouded in grey isolation while the rest of the world may be bathed in brilliant sunshine.

The mountains start at once on the south shore of the lake. The bumping and shuddering of the aircraft increases as we follow one of the black snakes of Whitton Creek. Sometimes the bulk of the river will be white and frozen and laced with glacier-green canyons, but on this trip a lot of the water is open. I can imagine the slow, painful slog through the soggy snow below and the agonising wade I would

have to make if the river crossing were not yet frozen.

On a calm day, Floyd would be flying lower, checking the chutes surrounding Avalanche Lake for moose feeding on the willows brought within their reach by the dumped snow, or scanning the rocks above them for goats. And if he saw them, he would stand the plane on a wing and zoom close so that his passengers could get a better look—whether they wanted one or not! And on a calm day, we would then have to soar suprisingly high to clear the steep wall at the head of this valley to reach my lake. But turbulent weather dictates a higher altitude and today the amoeboid sheet in its high, wide valley is visible before we leave Charlotte Lake. The mountains surrounding it are blurring and fading and the main divide beyond is swallowed in a black pall of cloud. Sporadic snowflakes streak like tracer past the windshield. High as we are, we still drop with a sharp bang as we cross the final barrier before the lake. I am always amazed at the rigidity of air; even a truck on a rocky road rides more smoothly.

The engine pitch changes and the virginal expanse of white wobbles up to meet us. The plane touches the surface but we skim along with very little lessening of speed then sway back into the air again. Floyd checks the skid marks for the dark stripe that would indicate overflow. The blue-black, snow-freckled forest tilts as we bump slowly round in a curve and Floyd must be satisfied for he continues to swing until he is pointing into the wind again and drops once more towards the ice. This time he throttles down and slews round in a blur of surface blizzard between the islands. I at once look at the cabin as it flashes into view but, from this distance, everything seems to be in order. As the motor is shut off, the demons which make my life so unpleasant both before and during a flight, flee instantly and I am suddenly enormously exhilarated. The high I get upon landing is almost worth the agonies of the flight itself.

The first load of supplies is dumped a good hundred yards from the cabin to avoid the greater risk of overflow close to the rocks along the shore. There are about six inches of loose snow on the lake and the surface is good but the instant I hit the shore I flounder in above my knees. The belly-flop ski track of an otter coils among the lakeside boulders. On with the snowshoes and I waddle to the door. The wire still snubs the wooden bolt tight and, inside, although a fair scattering of mouse droppings decorate the counter, nothing is amiss. A strike of a match ignites the prepared fire in the barrel stove. A metal bucket stands by it; a quick swipe in a snowbank to fill it and it is put on top of the drum.

The warm front which I had cursed while in the air has one advantage. The temperature is so close to freezing that the perishable food will need no protection other than the cardboard walls of its cartons until I can get it inside. In bitter weather I would have kept my sleeping bags handy in the plane and swathed the boxes with them until they reached the protection of the cabin. The barrel stove warms the cabin quickly and, before Floyd returns, a batch of bread has been started and the melted snow on the stove, pine needles, bits of bark and all, has been converted to a fragrant pot of tea.

I have known Floyd for some years. He is not a talkative man. We stand beside the second pile of freight. It is possible that friends might visit during the next three months, but some winters I have been alone for many weeks without seeing another soul. Floyd might be the last person with whom I speak for some time.

"Enjoy the party tonight," I say.

"Oh," he replies, smiling, "I've no doubt I will."

I clutch a couple of light items which sit on top of the freight pile and grab hold of the dogs to keep them away from the prop. There is a deafening roar as the motor is fired. Friction from the skis has melted the snow and they are now frozen to the ice, which begins to vibrate furiously beneath my feet. But the plane rocks and the skis suddenly jerk free. I bow my back against the snow flung up by the propeller, then the plane is leaping along the lake and lifting towards the storm. It gains altitude and curves slowly back overhead, and the red wings waggle slightly in farewell. It dips over the ridge at the foot of the lake and its sound is abruptly cut off by the swell of land.

The restless air soughs in the pines and flakes of snow tumble with the wind. I am alone and the wilderness is my own. I load the toboggan and begin to trudge towards the cabin.

## chapter 11

# how to make life difficult for yourself without really trying

*"Cheshire Puss," she began somewhat timidly,——"Would you please tell me which way to go from here?"*

*"That depends a good deal on where you want to get to," said the cat.*

*"I don't much care where——" said Alice.*

*"Then it doesn't matter which way you go," said the cat.*

*"——so long as I get somewhere," Alice added as an explanation.*

*"Oh you're sure to do that," said the cat, "if you only walk long enough."*

Lewis Carroll, *Alice in Wonderland*

I always used to travel on foot back and forth to the road but early winter weather has given me a couple of warnings I cannot ignore. Also, the brutal punishment I have sometimes endured is not as much fun as it used to be. So even though my brain screams at me to do anything—*anything* —except get into that plane, it is now the way I usually come home in winter.

The worst hike I ever made was in the middle of one November. I was leaving home and going outside to Nimpo. At that time of year, the most sensible route would have been to follow the river down to Charlotte Lake then fight the twelve miles of windfall along the shore to the ranch where my truck was stored. There was some snow around my cabin but I would likely run out of it lower down and the trip would pose few problems. It would, however, be bedeviled by windfall and be excessively swampy, wet and wearying. The peaks were thoroughly white above the tree line and the normal route over the west side of Halfway Mountain might well have some avalanche risk. But Bob Cohen's horse trail, which also went to the ranch, cut around the east side of the mountain and that would be free from slides. Although I would not have chosen the horse trail in summer, for it, too, was swampy and brushy, these difficulties would now be negated by the snow at that altitude, and it seemed a far more attractive prospect than the river.

In summer I would reach that trail by going round over my bridge, but that would give me an extra five miles of exposed conditions that I could avoid if I went down the river as far as an old cabin built by the

TRAP CABIN

Chris Czajkowski

original trapper, Sam Sulin. I could spend the night there and see what the weather was like the following morning. If the tops were clear I could go straight up the valley side and head for the horse-trail route, otherwise I would continue down through the swamps and windfalls. Judging by what I could see from below, the horse trail already had enough snow to warrant packing a toboggan and snowshoes along.

There was a warm and gusty southwest wind during the night at Sam's cabin, but there was no precipitation. I breakfasted by candle-light in order to be ready with the dawn and to make maximum use of the short November day. As soon as the trees began to separate themselves from the darkness, I walked down to the river to check on the peaks. The wind was obviously blowing pretty hard up top for it had stirred a ground blizzard that hung like gauze over the summits. I could not see the mountain I would have to climb as I was too close to the bottom of it, but, despite its haziness, the nameless peak on the far side of the valley was visible and I assumed the conditions on both would be much the same. Although the wind might be of storm force, it would be at my back and if it changed direction it would also slack off. Fair enough, I would try for the horse trail.

First there was the steep climb up the side of the valley, but I had brushed out the route when I first came into the country and the hike was not difficult. There had been no snow at all on the ground around Sam's cabin but a thin, patchy covering soon appeared. Initially, it made little difference to the ease of the climb but, about three quarters of the way to the tree line, the bush began to open out into alpine meadows, the wind grew stronger and the snow suddenly became deeper. Time to put on extra clothing and rearrange the outfit so that the toboggan did some of the work. (It is just a cheap, plastic child's sled, which I find as effective as anything, and which is also very light to carry when it cannot be used.)

A toboggan is not a particularly efficient tool for uphill travel—its advantages are on the flat or going down. The deepening snow and increased steepness of the slope made the next section pretty slow going. But I knew that once I topped the shoulder of the valley, the country would level out for the next two or three miles.

I should have turned back the instant I rounded the shoulder. I could still see the peak opposite, but the white, rock-streaked flanks of Halfway Mountain swept upward into a featureless grey pall. Underfoot, the snow was deep and soft and, now that the country was less sheltered, the wind was fierce. However, I had expended considerable energy in getting that far and the thought of going back down and facing the damp, dreary river trip after all was not appealing. I was still making progress: I would continue a little more—I could always turn back if it got worse.

I had been over the horse trail only once before and remembered it to be indistinct for the most part, particularly over the pass itself. But that was of no great concern. The trail was ill-defined because none of the long ridge that it traversed was difficult to cross and the horses spread out all over the place. The valley on the far side of the ridge housed my summer trail and I knew it well; the slopes leading down to it were not precipitous, nor was the bush impossibly dense. Once the top was reached, no matter where, all I would have to do was go down.

So on I went. Although a few pines still clothed the valley sides, the wide floor became tree-less. The wind buffeted but stayed at my back. Beneath the snow lay large areas of swampy meadows and partially frozen lakes whose ice might have been useful in places but there were too many suspect areas this early in the year to make them worth the risk. The meadows were not short-turfed and alpine but tussocky with sedge and liberally endowed with patches of scrub birch. Over this the snow had drifted with deceptive smoothness and every few steps I crashed into tight thickets of branches from which it was extremely energy-consuming to shake the snowshoes free. Without the webs, however, progress was even more difficult. But I knew these conditions would last only a mile or two and I struggled on. The dogs, each with their own pack, trudged miserably behind, snow blown deep into their fur and their tails jammed between their legs. Lonesome endured it with her usual reproachful silence and Sport whimpered and whined as he was prone to do in conditions he did not like. Occasional gusts punched like a fist and flung the toboggan in cartwheels in front of me.

The largest lake in this high, exposed valley is known locally as Fish Lake. It is big enough for a plane to land on and has surprisingly large trout for such a high altitude so has therefore become a summer tourist destination. It is from Fish Lake where the horse trail begins to climb to the ridge.

At first, despite the increased slope, the going was a little easier. The snow was no less deep, but the scrub birch and swamp had given way to a firmer substrate beneath scattered open pines. It was not cold but the snow had become coarse, like sugar, and the sled grated hard on this surface, a deadweight hanging on my hips. The wind buffeted and roared, but I wasn't being blown over and I'd survived such wind speeds before.

And I couldn't be too far off now. A half mile more, another hour at most, and I would be over the top. I could not imagine that conditions would get a great deal worse. But when the trees petered out, I was swallowed in a wild grey torment and the wind was a demon out of hell. It was not just the banshee screaming which was so stupefying, but the pounding against the hood of my jacket. The fabric rattled like twin kettle drums in my ears. The wind must surely have reached hurricane speeds.

Indistinct shapes in various degrees of grey and white loomed in the cloud. But distances were impossible to judge and the shadows might have been car-sized boulders or great chunks of mountain. Any signs of the trail had long disappeared. A vague, misshapen rise undulated ahead. The insane screaming and pounding was disorientating. I began to doubt, and doubt brought fear. This was insanity; suicidal. I was too puny to cope with such extreme forces. Resolve was draining away. But it was so close: so close. One foot stumbled after the other on the unevenly drifted ground. A few more agonising steps, another weary heave at the toboggan, and I made the top of the rise. In front of me was a solid grey nothing. And the maniacal screech and pummel of the wind. At my feet, the land sloped gently downwards for a short distance before disappearing. Was this the pass or just a small rise on the way? How idiotic to come this way in these conditions without being more certain of my route. I was chilling rapidly as I tried to think. Hypothermia sat grinning at my back. I once found a toad in a dried-out meadow in the fall. Its limbs were stretched in an attitude of walking, but it was dead, completely desiccated like the frost-burned sedges it had been trying to cross. I imagined myself like that toad; legs spread for the next step, back bowed, leaning against the pull of the toboggan, frozen in mid-stride until the winds thinned my body to a fine sliver like an icicle that doesn't drip but simply wears away in the cold. It was suicidal to stay here: lunacy to attempt to climb farther into the greyness. No matter where I was, I would have to go down.

The snow in the lee of the ridge was deeper and softer than ever. But gravity was on my side and within moments I was in the partial shelter of a small gully and the wind was reduced to a more tolerable level. Down I slithered through the waist-deep powder and soon the hunched gnomes of sub-alpine fir clumped together sufficiently to provide areas of comparative calm. Then a faint lightness appeared down below. A break in the cloud? But no; two distinct greynesses emerged divided by a solidly drawn edge. One side would be bush and the other snow-covered ice. I tried to picture Maydoe Creek with its string of lakes along which ran my summer trail, and fit the pattern to them. But in my heart I knew all along what it must be. I had not made the pass; the ridge had been merely an intermediate lift of the land; the wind, still at my back, had been deflected by the lie of the land; the gully had brought me back down to Fish Lake.

There was a very subtle but sudden alteration in the quality of the light. Even on thickly cloudy days, it is possible to notice when the sun goes down. I was surprised, for I had not thought I had been travelling for so long. But there was no doubt about it, it was growing darker by the minute.

Time to make camp. At least with snow in winter there is never any need to search for water. I chose the densest balsam clump I could find and crawled underneath. I never carry a tent in winter—a fire and a clump of bushes as a windbreak is much warmer—but I have a sleeping bag cover and an old small tent fly I use as a tarp; this last I arranged as best I could as an extra buffer against the storm. The dogs were exhausted and curled up at once in the snow. I scrounged for twigs and made a fire in a cave of branches for supper and tea. I was too weary to eat much; in any case, I had packed for a three-day trip and, as this was already my second night out, it didn't hurt to be cautious with food. I had probably covered six map miles during the day but, because I had swung round in the fog, I was perhaps less than four from where I had started. Darkness came while I ate and I fed the dogs and crawled into my sleeping bag.

I was tired enough to sleep at once but when I woke it was still completely dark. The wind continued to blow, although not as severely, but I could hear the hiss of gusting snow. Lying there alone, high on the wind-honed mountain, drowning under the snow-choked sky, was one of the few times I have been seriously frightened. I tried to suppress it but the thought that I might not get away with it this time continued to pick away at my brain. I have often been scared in the bush but usually whatever causes the fright is so sudden I don't have time to think about it and almost before I have registered the fear, the danger is gone. This time, though, there was nothing to do but worry, and wait.

My main concern (second to surviving at all) was that I would be overdue at Nimpo. As a safety measure I always gave my arrival date to Gloria and Roger Folsom at Wilderness Rim Resort where at that time I stayed outside on mail trips. They knew to wait twenty-four hours after I was overdue to allow for inclement weather before alerting the police, but I did not want to initiate a search unless I really needed it, otherwise in a real emergency my credibility might be compromised. Scared though I might be, I was neither lost nor hurt, and was not yet in need of help. In any case, even if a search were launched, no one would know where to look for me. Only Bob and Francie had any notion of where my routes might be—and they would probably compliment me with having enough sense to stay down by the river at this time of year. And Bob and Francie themselves would have to be found— they also lived without a phone in the bush and, as it was neither trapping nor hunting season, they might easily be out of the area entirely.

The shortest distance to any means of communication was still across the pass to the ranch where I had left my truck; if the morning was somehow miraculously clear and calm, I might just try it again. Even if I did not reach Nimpo in time, the caretaker at the ranch had a radiophone and I could at least call out.

A second choice would be to return over the scrub-birch swamps and go back down to Sam's cabin, then follow the river as I should have done in the first place. Once I dropped over the shoulder of land there would be little difficulty. But the two miles of scrub birch would be a hefty obstacle if the wind did not change, for it would be blowing directly into my face. I did not think I would have either the physical or mental reserves to fight it.

A third option was to follow the Fish Lake river out. It serviced a different watershed than the Whitton Creek complex and ran through another mile or so of open country before tumbling down into the McLinchy river. I was aware that there was a trail along the McLinchy somewhere, for Bob had talked about it, but I had never been in that direction. If it was anything like the other trails in the area, it would not exactly qualify as a major highway. Somewhere at the end of it was a logging road that came out on the highway about twenty miles south of Nimpo Lake.

Although I was beginning to wonder if the earth had somehow stopped turning during the night, dawn finally came. The prognosis was not hopeful. My body blended with the landscape, mummified under several inches of fresh snow, and the dogs were nowhere to be seen until they stirred and shook themselves. The sky was thick and grey and full of whirling flakes. The wind had lessened a little during the small hours but by the time I had loaded my gear, it was swelling forth again. The pass and Sam's cabin were out; the McLinchy it would have to be.

There was still a mile of open country to negotiate and it seemed endless. Even with snowshoes I sank thigh-deep with every step. Finally I reached the trees. Which side of the creek would the trail follow? Snow falling horizontally had plastered the vegetation and if there were any trail blazes at all they were hidden. I tried to think like a horse and scanned the forest for any openings that looked suitable for a pack-train. But at the edge of the tree line there are always many openings; I would simply have to bush bash and hope I hit something more recognisable in due course.

I had thought that the forest might be easier to walk through but, although it sheltered me from the storm, the snow within was softer than ever. It was waist deep and too loose for snowshoes to be a lot of help and I frequently took them off and waded. Neither method of progress was faster, but each type of struggle used different muscles and gave the others a respite. I tried one side of the creek then, as the bush grew denser and the trees themselves became obstacles as well as the snow, I crossed to the other. But of a trail there was no sign and progress was excruciatingly slow. Because of the shelter and loss of altitude, the temperature rose slightly and the snow became wet and heavy, which added to the chore of floundering through it. Finally I opted for the creek-bed itself. Parts of it were open and parts snow-bridged, but at least it took a fairly straight and comparatively open passage through the bush. Sometimes I could move quite well for several yards on the snow bridges but I never knew when I was going to break through or how deep the water would be underneath. At steeper places small falls tumbled over naked rocks and I slithered directly down these. My felt-lined boots were squelching with water and I was saturated from the rib cage down. My load was on my back again—the toboggan was useless in this—and I was carrying Lonesome's little pack as well for she looked ready to give up. She has never liked water or wet snow, and I would heave myself along for several yards then turn around to find that she had not followed. I would have to yell myself hoarse before she finally stirred. Sport was also doing a lot of yelling and crying every time he came to a creek crossing he thought he could not jump or some equally pathetic obstacle, but he was in fact a very able dog and could manage all sorts of difficult terrain quite easily.

For most of the day, two miles was all I could cover. The third mile I did in an hour for finally I hit easier going and as I slithered down between the trees the snow rapidly became less deep. And a little before the ground levelled off somewhat I saw a blaze, and then another: it was the trail.

I might have had another hour of daylight to play with but I was extremely tired and very wet. I made camp under a big spruce and collected a good pile of fuel for the fire as I had some serious drying out to do; however that operation was only marginally successful for I kept falling asleep and there was not a garment or a sleeping bag that did not end up falling into the fire. Ripstop nylon might be just the fabric for the average high-tech hiker, but it has only to look at a flame to dissolve.

It took four and a half days to cover the distance from Fish Lake to the logging road—I later met hikers who had completed the trip, in summer, in one. The trail was as difficult to follow as I had feared. There was little sign of it on the ground and snow had plastered the up-river sides of the trees so that visible blazes were few and far between. After each of the many little clearings I would have to walk a little way into the forest along the likeliest route then look behind me to see if I was going in the right direction. If I could see no blazes, I would use precious time and energy casting about until I spotted them. I knew from experience that any kind of trail was better than none—if I simply floundered somewhere in the direction in which the river was going I would likely end up bluffed or in bad windfall or an old burn and be a great deal worse off.

The lack of food did not worry me greatly for I knew that both I and my dogs had more than enough subcutaneous reserves to weather a few days on short rations. The last two suppers consisted of three slices of bread; one for each dog and one for myself; I had the advantage of hot water and a little weak tea. Dehydration was more of a problem than hunger, for I did not want to waste time melting water during the day and, along the trail, which was some distance above the river, there were no open creeks. The energy to tramp down to the river and back could not be spared, and eating snow is the surest way for the body to squander vital calories in an emergency. Despite large quantities to drink both morning and night, I was always thirsty. (Oddly enough, dogs seem unaffected by eating snow; in fact, even when given the choice, mine rarely drink liquids in winter.)

I had been walking for two or three hours on the sixth day after leaving home when I finally reached a fence. Remnants of a cleared area, once logged and now grazed, stretched ahead. There had to be some kind of vehicle track servicing it. I was, by my calculations, three days overdue. It was imperative that I reach a phone as soon as possible.

The logging road ran smack through the middle of it. It was four miles more to the highway, but by now the snow was little more than ankle deep and the flat surface and absence of windfall made the rest of the walk seem easy. Just before I reached the highway, I heard a deep-throated vehicle moving slowly. A grader ploughing the road! I ran the last stretch and flagged him down. He called his headquarters on his CB radio and they phoned Gloria and Roger at Wilderness Rim; within an hour I was sitting in their kitchen. And then I found out that, while still at home, I had lost track of the date. I was three days out in my calculations. Instead of being overdue, I had arrived at Nimpo exactly on time.

No one had worried about me at all.

The second time the weather showed me what it could do was in a November of a different year. I had arrived at Nimpo on the twenty-sixth, having gone down the river in the usual way and without mishap. There were already a couple of feet of snow at home, but at Charlotte Lake, and at Nimpo, only a few inches covered the ground. The day I arrived, snow began to blow and the prospect looked miserable—I was glad I would have a roof over my head that night.

I was tired and went to bed early. Roger was down at the coast helping his son and Gloria was janitoring at the Anahim school until 10:00 PM; she later told me that, although it was still snowing steadily when she came home, the graders were working and she had had no difficulty with the road.

The ploughs apparently gave up at about 2:00 AM; come daylight, there were two feet of snow on the ground and the flakes were coming down so thickly it was impossible to see across the yard. There was not a breath of wind. The three or four vehicles scattered about Gloria's yard disappeared in front of our eyes. The only visible item on my old red Dodge Powerwagon was the radio aerial; otherwise, it was completely buried.

Neither Gloria nor I had seen anything like it. It quit, later that day, when it was four feet deep. Forty-eight inches had fallen in twenty-four hours. The Folsoms were so little used to such large quantities of snow that Gloria phoned her husband down at the coast to ask him where the snow shovels were. "The only one we have is bust," he said. "Go to the store and get another."

"Roger," Gloria countered, "We can't *get* to the store."

The driveway of the Wilderness Rim Resort is perhaps quarter of a mile long. It took the two of us two hours to break trail to the road. Even with snowshoes we sunk to our waists. A single lane had been ploughed along the highway and, because less snow fell farther east, the road to Williams Lake was soon open. Bella Coola was cut off for a week.

If it had happened two days earlier, I would have been caught halfway down Whitton Creek. Travelling through it would have been next to impossible and I don't like to speculate on the result. I had planned on being at Nimpo for only a few days, but poor Gloria ended up putting up with me for over three weeks. Other neighbours from Charlotte lake were also stranded there for about ten days—we played an awful lot of cards. I tried at one point to hike back in, but gave up and returned to Nimpo. In the end, I waited for the ice to form and got Floyd to fly me home.

A woman and child died in that snow. The woman was from Alberta and she and her little boy had planned to visit family in Bella Coola. She had gassed up at Anahim the evening Gloria was working at the school, and that was the last time she and her son were seen alive. The following day, as soon as anyone could move, planes and dogs were sent out to search, but nobody really knew where to look. There are fifty miles of sparsely inhabited valley road and another forty at least where no one lives at all between Anahim and Bella Coola. The most rugged section comprises twenty miles of hairpin bends that drop four thousand feet down a cliff. Thirty avalanches had obliterated this part of the road and the victims might have been under any one of them, or have been pushed or driven off the road altogether—in many places it is single-lane and crumble-edged.

The woman and child were not found until the blade of the plough struck their vehicle. They had nearly made it to the bottom, they were still on the road, and all the avalanches had missed them. They had slid into the small ditch against the cliff and the woman must have panicked for three tires were burned out in her efforts to get free. It was not particularly cold, just around freezing, and either a fire outside or extra clothing in the car would have kept them warm. But the woman had run the car engine to keep the heater going and she and her child had died of carbon monoxide asphyxiation. When found, they were not even wearing their coats.

# chapter 12

# Was the stone-age ethical?

*What has happened will happen again*
*and what has been done will be done again*
*and there is nothing new under the sun.*

Ecclesiastes 1:9

A colossal roaring crash, like a dozen avalanches and the end of the world all rolled into one, dragged me out of sleep, fighting for my wits. Heart pounding like a sledgehammer, I knew what had caused it even before I was fully awake, but was unable to stop the adrenaline rush. Only those who have experienced it can possibly know what it is like to be inside a building with a metal roof when the snow slides off.

When I first arrived home at the beginning of the year, a pristine mop cap two-feet deep encased the cabin like a large, fluffy mushroom. But the mild weather and the warmth of the stove encouraged the chimney side to slide. Usually, only parts of it go at a time. It starts with a slow, muffled creaking that may go on for ten or fifteen minutes until a mind-numbing crash ensues; one thinks the lot has gone, but five minutes later *crick ... crick ... crickcrick* starts again until one's whole concentration is focused on it, waiting for it, and yet still the roar is a shock.

I had thought a metal roof pitched at a sixty-degree angle would have allowed the snow to slide easily and frequently, but it is surprising how it can stick. My rude awakening that January night was caused by all the chimney side of the building going at once. When I built the cabin, although I knew a snow pack of four to five feet could be expected, I had not allowed for the accumulation that would occur on the west side of the building. After all, when I stand on the ground in summer, I am unable to reach the bottoms of the rafters. But on that side of the cabin the ground slopes upwards and as the snow slides off it soon piles to the eaves. Further dumps have nowhere to go. When Nuk Tessli blows from the lake, drifting occurs as well and I have occasionally come home in winter to find the cabin buried to

the ridge pole. However, it always clears off on the chimney side sooner or later, so the building is sometimes subject to a lot of uneven weight for which it was not designed. The trap cabins all have such a list to one side that the doors no longer close and the walls need propping up with tree trunks. It is not the tilting of the building that worries me so much as what would happen to the foundations. The cabin supports are simply perched on whatever rocks were handy

*Chris Czajkowski*

but not actually attached to anything. I worried that the heavy pressure on one side of the building might push the whole thing down the hill. I once met a man who built a house which fell down after ten years; I have this figure in my mind and feel that if my building survives that long, it will handle most things.

But it might not get that far unless something was done about the uneven pressure on the roof. Despite an uncomfortably hot fire the following day, in the hopes that warm air would fill the attic and loosen the rest of the snow, it refused to go. There was plenty of space under the eaves at that stage for the snow was still all on the roof. The steepness of the metal defies any attempt to walk on it, so I dug out the ladder and lugged it round to the west side of the house. The ladder is home-made and, because of the stunted and twisted trees that were available to build it, cumbersome and somewhat short. The low snowpack under the eaves meant the ladder would not reach far. Snowshoes were jammed under the bottom rung to stop it falling further into the snow. (I learned that trick after once being left dangling by my fingers from the ridge cap while the ladder, felt for by my questing toes, promptly sank deeper and out of reach: I had to let myself drop blindly and hope for the best; fortunately, the best happened, but I had a really good fright.) Then, with a shovel, a very long arm and an inevitable quantity of snow down my sleeves and neck, the roof was cleared. It was already snowing heavily and more was piling up when I finished, but the pressure was off.


So far, I had always been around when the heaviest snow occurred, but since the craft-fair circuit took up the autumn and big dumps sometimes occurred then, I could not guarantee to be home at the crucial time. Just as I was working out in my mind how to deal with the problem, a young American couple dropped by on their way to Alaska. Dan and Rene Lemay had been corresponding with me for a couple of years since they read *Cabin at Singing River*, the story of the Atnarko venture (which they perused in Thailand, of all places!). They had just completed a log cabin building course in Penticton, and they were itching to try out their new-found skills.

As always, aestheticism was an important consideration in the

design of the additional supports. I did not want great heavy permanent buttresses restricting the view and looking ugly in summer, thus
we should have to devise something of a temporary nature. This meant
that while it had to be strong, it also had to be light enough for me to
erect and dismantle on my own. The structure was further dependent on what useful rocks we could find on the ground: to the lee of
the cabin the soil is mostly deep duff under a little thicket of balsam
firs and few boulders break the surface.

I was impressed with the carpentry tricks Dan and Rene had
learned on their course, many of which were really simple ideas, but
which I had not known about or figured out for myself. The resulting removable flying buttresses are elegant in the extreme; they, and
a pole woodshed that was constructed when two young women were
staying with me a few years back are the only projects for which I
have so far had help while building this place.

But although roof shoveling is no longer such an urgent concern,
that does not mean to say there is no more snow to manipulate. The
trails to the lake shore, the outhouse and between the cabins are simply dealt with: they are merely compacted by tramping back and forth
a few times, first wearing the snowshoes and then with boots. Within a
day or two they are firm enough to need little further attention except
a pass over with the snowshoes every time there is another fall.

By far the biggest shovelling job is banking the walls. I learned
from living at the Atnarko cabin that a lack of insulating snow around
the bottom logs of a building in winter makes a serious difference to
the warmth inside. Here, the four-foot drop below the foundations
on the east side of the building posed problems, but I figured if I
constructed a loose wall of odd slabs about a foot from the interior
basement wall, I could fill this with snow and it would work just as
well. Unfortunately, the supports for the walkway and deck that run
though this space make pushing snow down into it too difficult to
do properly and this cabin has never been as easy to keep warm as I
had hoped. When the weather is mild, this deficiency is not noticeable, but in cold spells the layer of chilled air that sits over the floor
inside can never be removed and anything left upon it will freeze.

Melting snow for water is perfectly possible, but a nuisance. There
is a constantly hissing bucket or washtub on the stove and, despite

the fact I must have eaten quantities of them in the dark while camping at various times, the added needles and bark scraps revealed in good light give pause for thought. So a hole in the ice covering the lake through which to draw water is fairly high on my list of priorities. I hack through the layers of frozen water with a chainsaw. This is an uncomfortably wet operation; once the bar cuts through the ice, gouts of water are driven upward by the chain. The force required to keep the bar cutting through the ice makes it very difficult to stand out of the way. The hole has to be made quite large for it freezes inwards as well as across the top and will rapidly shrink during cold spells. So a bucket-sized hole would be useless in a very short time and I usually start with one about three feet across; sometimes I have to enlarge it again with the chainsaw later through the winter.

There is one other shovelling job to complete before I am organised (and it doesn't take long so I usually do it right away) and that is the unearthing of the solar panels. The two small glass and silicone rectangles are bolted to a frame and light enough to lift. They are attached by a fifty-yard cord to the batteries and inverter so that, in winter they can be carried onto the ice to avoid the tree shadows that fall around the cabin. Even the shadow of a single twig can make a difference to the panels' efficiency.

The conversion of energy from one of its manifestations to another has always fascinated me. A leaf uses sunlight to make sugars; we can either consume these energy packs directly or ignite them to provide heat and light. We can also manipulate them further to convert them into that mysterious force that is electricity.

When I was four my parents moved the family to the tall, skinny, late-Victorian brick house in which I was to grow up. I dimly recall gas lamp brackets on the walls but electricity must have been put in very early and I don't remember life without it. The thought of not having it never even crossed my mind.

The wonder of electricity can truly be appreciated only by someone who makes their own. Generators do not appeal to me. They are hideously noisy, they consume fuel and, if such a machine went wrong here, it would be an extremely difficult and expensive item to get to a mechanic. Windmills are cheaper and snatch power from the air, but they, too, are noisy and their parts wear out and frequently break.

They are also not designed for the fierce storms that occur here several times a year. The cabin is too far from the nearest creek to make a water turbine practical and so solar power is the choice for me. And what a miraculous invention it is. Absolutely silent and odourless, there they sit, the two midnight-blue oblongs with their patterns of opalescent shards, endlessly converting the sun's effortlessly sustainable energy into push-button magic. No alchemist in his quest to turn base metals into gold ever imagined such a treasure as this. My panels are older models and not as efficient as others now available on the market, but this surely has to be the power of the future. It is our only resource that we can use without destroying (at our present level of technology). It is criminal that its capacity for development has been blocked by industrial empires constructed on the monopolization of fossil fuels and water.

Because of this technology's restricted development, my two old-fashioned panels and two six-volt, deep-cycle batteries do not provide enough power for the kind of household use most people expect. Anything which converts electricity into heat is particularly costly, which means dishwashers, driers, cookstoves, toasters, hot plates, coffee machines, irons (irons? Could I ever imagine one of those in my life?), hot water and baseboard heaters, and power tools would need much larger banks of panels and batteries. But many people run houses full of appliances with solar energy, with perhaps a generator for peak-use backup. The initial outlay is expensive but, apart from the replacement of the batteries every five to eight years, there are no fees to pay and no other running costs.

But I am not interested in most appliances. When I stay with friends outside, I am delighted to be able to use them, but here I do not miss them. I prefer to spend my money on more interesting things. It is not that I consider manual work to be part of the mythology of wilderness living; far from it: I am just as lazy as the next person. But I accept physical chores without really thinking about them as simply par for the course, in the same way that a city dweller puts up with daily commutes, unmitigated mechanical noise, time wasted in lineups, and the ritualized locking of doors.

I do not even use the power for lights. There are power-efficient light bulbs on the market but, during long dull spells of weather, I require every once of energy that my system can produce. I need it to run a computer.

"But what," is the inevitable reaction, "do you want a computer *for?*"

It is traditional in western culture to consider animists, those people who invest trees and rocks and other objects with spiritual properties, as quaint. And yet our materialistic culture is loaded with allegorical interpretation. The wilderness itself, in city-speak, represents purity, simplicity (which it isn't) and a sort of anthropomorphic moral (if not intellectual) superiority. The computer, by standing at the head of our technological evolution, is symbolic of the development of industry and, by implication, the ruination of that wilderness: therefore, despite its universal use in one form or another, the computer has become immoral. Because whole nations have been extinguished by technological advancement that destroyed their environments, one might go so far as to add genocide to the computer's record of crimes.

Then there is a more subtle association to people's astonishment at the presence of a computer in the wilderness. Wilderness dwellers are expected to exist on mountain dew and be intellectually stimulated by nothing more than the contemplation of their navel. They are expected to be mystical rather than practical, and to maintain their equilibrium with a spiritual instinct rather than by a conscious manipulation of the brain cells. If that is the case, the city person reasons, why would a wilderness dweller need such a sophisticated tool?

Anyone who has read this far into the book has presumably enjoyed it. Which no one would be able to do if the publisher had decided not to publish it. And, I can assure you, it is hard enough to persuade a publisher to look at a manuscript, even when it is neatly presented on impeccably typed, immaculately clean paper and accompanied by the mandatory computer disc. How far would I get if I sent it to him written on birch bark with a goose feather quill dipped into huckleberry juice? (Which, incidentally, would fade long before he got around to reading it.)

There will still be those who condemn the computer as a betrayal of their wilderness ideal. Consider, then, the symbolism associated with other writing tools: the portable typewriter, the ball-point pen, and the feather, or indeed any type of tool at all. The typewriter would be more acceptable to the romanticized version of the wilderness, but that device is in itself a result of quite an advanced technology. Even a humble feather pen has technological modifications. Where does technology begin and end? Why is an axe more acceptable to the city-dweller's image of wilderness compatibility than a chainsaw? An axe, moreover, that is made of steel. Was a metal cutting edge not just as great an innovation for its time as the capsule that took men to the moon is in ours? Was the first person who bound a sharp rock to a stick condemned as a heretic? Probably, to some degree, for resistance to change is imbedded in all of us.

But back to writing tools. A computer, you will say, is different from the others because it uses electricity. But are the sun's only worthy uses those of making suntans and growing vegetables? Is the energy not there for whoever can make use of it? The panels themselves, and the inverter and the batteries, as well as the computer and printer, have to be made in factories, and presumably these all have some environmental cost. But so do typewriters. And ball-point pens.

Using the computer cannot separate me from the rhythms of nature. For much of the year this is a sunny environment and I can do all the typing I need without much problem. Even during dull spells, two fully charged six-volt, deep-cycle batteries will keep me going for a couple of days. But when it snows continuously I must brush the panels frequently and, when I am really desperate, must move them around to catch every gleam of sunshine within the limitations of the cord. If all else fails, I simply have to turn my attention elsewhere; there are always exciting activities like income tax forms to fill in. (I still have to go through the motions, even if I never actually pay any.)

As I write, it is still dark outside. I am a morning person and in the winter I often work for several hours before daylight emerges. The computer screen would be too glaring on its own and besides, it does not light the keyboard which, in ergonomically expedient fashion, is placed on a rough, hand-sawn board a few inches lower than the work bench on which the computer rests. (For years a log round with a cushion on top did duty as a seat; recently I have acquired a cast-off office chair complete with swivel stem and wheels and am feeling very grand.) As I need every scrap of electricity in winter for writing, I cannot spare any power for lights so kerosene lamps and candles are used to illuminate the keyboard.

In daylight, the window behind the screen looks onto the lake. At night, the combined efforts of screen and lamps give a subtle glow which fails to eradicate the dark. High in the centre of the window, this January morning, is the planet Jupiter, unusual in its brightness this year. Some distance below and to the east, a dimmer star has risen, and this is a sign that very soon daylight will colour the world. (How many city folk, I wonder, can watch the stars wheeling behind their computer screens?)

It is an absolutely clear night and the sunrise this morning will be spectacular. Just before it hits the mountains they will turn a ghostly pale with purplish sky behind. Suddenly the range will switch on a startling pink, a jagged neon sign hung disembodied between the purplish sky and earth. The light will strengthen and the mountains will run the gamut of orange, through gold, to blinding white then POP! Fingers of sunshine will reach across the lake and fling themselves into my windows.

And out on the ice the silicone molecules in the solar panels will jiggle and dance power back into the system, so I can encode these lines on a floppy disc and send them to the publisher, who, if I am lucky, will feed them into *his* computer, then send them to the printer's computer to be preserved on film for posterity.

# chapter 13

## *neighbours*

*But my old friend ...had told me: "The person who can take delight in a sweet tune without wanting to learn it, in a beautiful woman without wanting to possess her, or in a magnificent head of game without wanting to shoot it, has not got a human heart." So that the shot ... (to kill the lion) was in reality a declaration of love ...*

Isak Dinesen, *Out of Africa*

The attempt to make an income from the craft-fair circuit achieved only moderate success—it rarely produced anywhere near that which I had earned tree-planting—and it brought with it an additional problem. I had been enthusiastic in stocking my booth and now I was left with tons of unsold artwork, made even bulkier because of the matting. To make matters worse, when I paint, I like to paint big.

I had to find somewhere to store all this worthless paper. Gloria and Roger had continued to be wonderful hosts but my possessions in their attic were becoming an embarrassment and I looked around the Nimpo area for a suitable building, preferably one graced with a stove so that I could stay in it when going out to do mail. Needless to say, with a breadline existence, cost was of prime importance. Many people would have given me a free cabin as long as I needed it only during the winter, but it would have been expensive—and pointless— to fly all those pulped trees into the mountains in the spring and back out to Nimpo in the fall.

Mary Kirner has owned the Nimpo Lake Resort, which is situated halfway between Nimpo and Anahim, for twenty-six years. I had heard a lot about Mary, although I had not spoken to her much, and was somewhat aware of her easygoing and philanthropic nature, but was totally unprepared for her instant warm friendship and the delight I would have in subsequently knowing her. Mary's simple solution to life is to give and she has an unending supply of uncomplicated generosity for whoever happens to cross her path. She loves flowers and has filled her house with a brilliant, exotic jungle, an extraordinary contrast to the harsh landscape outside when the thermometer hits fifty below. Ducks and geese and rabbits and peacocks and funny-looking chickens run about the property to the delight of all who stay there, including, I am afraid to say, my dogs.

Mary, however, is not just a resort-owner: she is an institution. When the restaurant at Nimpo had to be sold, she could not bear to see it empty and she took it over. When the store no longer wished to handle the post office, Mary took that under her wing as well. Over the years other people have built cabins and retirement homes close to her own, and every single occupant has become family. One of her resort cabins is winterised and, because it is only six miles from the store and the post office in one direction, and the school and therefore the photocopier in the other, and is surrounded by a veritable hotbed of telephones and fax machines, my cabin on Mary's resort has become my townhouse.

Nick Christiansen, Mary's partner, is an aircraft afficionado and is one of several neighbours who owns a plane. (Nimpo Lake has been dubbed the floatplane capital of B.C.) Since I have become part of Mary's extended family, my winters at Nuk Tessli have changed. I used to spend up to six or seven weeks at a stretch without any contact with the outside world, which was the longest I felt I could go without dealing with the mail—or going squirrelly; then I would make a mid-winter trip to the outside. I would stay a few days to organise business, then trek back in again. A few of these hikes were fairly easy, but many involved a great deal of hard slogging and discomfort. Although, by mid-February, the snow and ice were usually in better condition than earlier in the winter, it could still be very cold; conversely, due to the capriciousness of coastal weather, I have been rained on a couple of times during February: bottomless, rain-soaked, rotten snow is the devil to travel through.

But now I seldom hike back and forth during the winter. Every three or four weeks either Nick and Mary or one of the other neighbours drops by for coffee and, as well as mail, they often bring unimaginable treats to which I would normally not have access; salad greens, fruit, jugs of liquid milk, and a collection of funny-looking eggs from Mary's funny-looking chickens. I never know when anyone is coming and they naturally choose pleasant weather, the same conditions which tend to entice me on longer hikes, consequently I am not always home. I will hear the plane come and go when I am out in the bush, or even see it if I am above the tree line or in the middle of one of the lakes, but I do not attempt to hurry back for I know they will be long gone before I can return. The note on the door will inform them of my whereabouts and the warmth of the stove will indicate that I am still of this world. They will find the outgoing mail hung on a nail beside the door and, as I happily tramp homeward, I am gleefully anticipating the surprises that will be in store for me. I feel a bit uncomfortable with this unsolicited largess on the part of the neighbours, but they always maintain they enjoy having an excuse to get out in their airplanes; it is also a pretty good feeling to know that they are keeping a collective eye on me.


My wild neighbours keep a sharp watch on me as well, although no doubt for very different reasons. The Atnarko River, where I used to live, was a much better place to observe wildlife than up here at Nuk Tessli. Down below, both the annual feast of spawning salmon and the open river during the winter attracted a wide variety of creatures—grizzly bears would feed in the river right in front of my deck. But here food is scattered and there are few incentives for animals to congregate; nonetheless, it is amazing how many creatures do inhabit this comparatively Spartan area. They are seldom seen or heard;

without the white notebook of the snow I would have very little idea that they existed.

During warm spells small groups of birds flit companionably through the forest—pine siskins and mixed flocks of mountain chickadees and nuthatches mostly. They systematically search the bark cracks and lichens on the trees for insects. I can't see a sign of anything there but the birds find plenty to keep them busy. They disappear as the weather becomes cooler (where do they go?) presumably because the insects they feed on retreat farther into their shelters to avoid freezing.

Another common neighbour is the thrush-sized pine grosbeak with its rosy cape and soft, bubbly calls rather like the bird whistles I used to blow into water as a kid. Hairy woodpeckers give their periodic piercing whistles and whack tree trunks with measured, axe-like blows. Once in a while, before the lake freezes, trumpeter swans pause for a while, but there is no feed for them when the ice begins to form and they soon depart for the coast. The ptarmigan's calligraphy always amuses me. Their bodies cleave a trough and their feather snowshoes waddle from side to side so closely within it that the mark resembles a tiny track from a vehicle doing doughnuts as the bird feasts off the shoreline alder buds sticking above the snow. If the snow lies loosely on the lake and there is no wind, small holes will appear scattered here and there well away from the shore. No tracks lead to them, but a closer look will show a skid before them containing one or two footprints, and fragile patterns of wing beats immediately after them. These are little self-dug caves where the ptarmigan spend the night. When the snow on the lake is wind packed, they roost in the wells beneath trees but they invariably seek the lake if conditions are right—they must feel safer out in the open.

By far the most noticeable bird in the neighbourhood, both winter and summer, is the Clarks nutcracker. A member of the crow family, *Nucifraga* looks quite a bit like a whiskeyjack but is a little larger and has a bold white rump and black wings, and also a much longer beak. This invaluable tool is used to rip apart pine cones to get at the seeds. The fruit it does not at once eat, it packs off and caches in loose soil for use as winter fodder. Apparently, temporary caches are made close to the source, but as much of the ground around my

CLARKS NUTCRACKER

cabins will be buried under at least four feet of snow for five months of the year, most of the soil the bird ultimately chooses will be high above the tree line on exposed ridges. When I first hiked these mountains I was very curious about some hard seed cases, not unlike those of a small-pea-sized hazelnut, littering the highest peaks, at least fifteen hundred feet above the tree line. They were obviously far too large to have come from any nearby plant, all of which were less than a hand's breadth in height. Had *people* been up here and left the debris of some exotic nut with which I was unfamiliar? Not impossible, but there could not have been many human visitors, for this area is rarely visited by tourists—and it seemed odd that every intruder would leave such quantities of the same kind of garbage!

When I came to Nuk Tessli, I was aware that the forest was pine and that it was much contorted, but did not know that two species of *Pinus* interact here, one the more familiar lodgepole and the other the far more unusual whitebark pine *(Pinus albicaulis*— not to be confused with the very different western white pine, *Pinus monticola)*. The whitebark is a high altitude tree only and, instead of more traditional cones which open to allow winged seeds to fly away, it bears a structure not unlike a pitch-daubed hand grenade. Inside the thick, resinous bracts are brown, wingless seeds. They are Canada's very own pine nut.

The interesting thing about the cone is that it apparently never opens unaided. Its oil-rich fruit is much sought after by squirrels and birds and even grizzly bears who, like the natives used to, acquire the nuts by digging up the squirrel's underground storage middens. To try and defend itself the cone has evolved its massive, permanently closed bracts, but in that state, paradoxically, it is no longer able to germinate. The very animals it has tried to forestall are its only salvation. How many seeds the squirrels fail to eat and thus liberate I don't know but probably not many for such rich provender would be consumed very quickly. However, the main animal involved with the procreation of this tree is the Clark's nutcracker.

Candace Savage, in *Bird Brains* (Toronto, 1995), maintains that the crow is considered the most intelligent of birds, and the nutcracker the most intelligent of crows. They apparently home in on their caches by taking bearings off nearby prominent features, which must be quite large to defeat the winter covering, and can unearth caches buried under four feet of snow. Niko Tinbergen in *A Curious Naturalist* (Boston, 1984) observed this behaviour with sand wasps who came back repeatedly to concealed burrows in which they laid their eggs, bearing live, paralyzed insects to bury beside their larvae as a food supply. If Tinbergen removed cones or stones from the surrounding area and replaced them in the same pattern a few inches away, the wasp would home in on the markers and be unable to find its brood.

Animal intelligence is qualified in laboratories by tests determining the subject's ability to recognize symbols and relate them to food. This is directly linked to memory, otherwise feeding would simply be at random. The crow-family's intelligence, however, was a puzzle for biologists at first, for mammalian memory is stored in the cortex and this part of the brain is poorly developed in birds. However, birds possess a hyperstriatum, which we do not have at all, and it is this which is responsible for avian memory. And if total brain size in relationship to that of its body is any indication of smarts, crows are right up there with dolphins and even the sapient Homo himself. "A single nutcracker," writes Savage, "is estimated to cache between 22,000 and 33,000 seeds in up to 7,500 different places" and apparently capitalizes upon at least half of them.

Well! As I have trouble remembering where I put anything without writing it down, it certainly shows where I fall on the intelligence scale. I feel quite humble when the bird acknowledges my intrusion into his domain and deigns to consume the fat I hang up for him in winter.

The majority of the mammalian tracks around my cabin belong to meat eaters. I hardly ever see any blood on the snow, so they must survive principally on mice (who live under the snow) and consume them out of sight. But this year, judging by the lack of scrabbles and rustling in the walls and ceiling of my cabin, mice are at the bottom of their cycle. Squirrels are not visible victims and rabbits are never plentiful up here, and yet I find footprints of marten, weasel and mink, the belly-flop ski marks of otters (although he will find plenty of fish), and once I followed the blurred meanderings of an animal which had paws as big as those of my larger dog but whose interval and depth was much less; I think it might have been a lynx. They were trapped lower down in the past, but I have never seen one.

But the most surprising tracks of all, in view of this seemingly foodless environment, are those of the wolves. When I first explored this lake, I came up the wall of the great trough in the west for I was still living in the Atnarko cabin. No one I knew had ever been that way and as far as I can determine, I am the only human that ever has. I picked a spur beside a steep little creek as it looked the most likely way up the wall and found that the animals had known of it long ago. A wide, deep game trail, rich with bear, deer, goat, moose and wolf tracks had been dug deeply into the spine of the spur. My lake and the branch of Whitton Creek that runs from it are part of this same major game route, one of the very few that joins the interior Chilcotin plateau to the coast. Human beings might well decide that the high, dry Interior and mild humid coast are separate ecosystems, but the animals know no such boundaries.

On one occasion, wolves had crossed the other end of my lake right after there had been a small skiff of snow during the night, so I knew the tracks had been made only hours before. The animals must have been fully aware of my presence, but were it not for the tell-tale snow I would never have known they had been by. There seemed to be quite a number in the pack but it was impossible to tell how many for they all placed their feet unerringly in the same holes in the snow that the leader had made, just as my dogs did after them. It is interesting watching a dog come upon a track—it seems likely that the wolf hunts in the same way. They trot along thinking of nothing in particular then suddenly, as the track comes within range, prick their ears forward then stuff their noses deep into a paw mark. A few muffled snorts in one or two places and they immediately look in the direction in which the creature has gone. How do they know this?

What signals are there in paw prints to tell them which way an animal is walking? It can't be visual otherwise they would not be able to figure it out in summer. And, although animal paws often contain scent glands, I've watched the dogs, when they cannot see me, behave in exactly the same way with my own footprints. Surely there is not much difference between the smell of the heel and the toe of my boot. After sniffing, the dogs often look both up and down the track. Can they detect anomalies in the scent of the air above it?

I skied by the wolf trail for quite a way through the forest. Apart from an occasional diversion to a tree from one or two members of their group, the animals had travelled with a single-minded efficiency on a route which used every contour of the land to save energy. Eventually the trail veered off by the outlet of my lake to follow the river down. They will no doubt hope to find moose and grouse and possibly caribou; there are active beaver dams down there, too, but the beaver pretty much stay below the ice in the winter and I don't know how much success the wolves would have with them. The pack is probably having a hard time in this low-snow year for their prey will be able to run. The wolves do better when the snow is deep and their quarry is soon exhausted.

No catalogue of my winter wildlife would be complete without the snow fleas. These belong to that vast category of animals, of whose worth we are only just beginning to be aware, those billions of minute organisms who live in and nurture the soil. Snow fleas are not a flea at all, but a springtail: the common name has been earned by their ability to jump several inches vertically into the air, no mean feat when you are the size of a pepper grain. They do this, not with their feet, but by locking their tails under hooks slung from their bodies, and suddenly releasing them.

The leaps are purely skywards and do not contribute to the animal's forward locomotion. For that, they crawl. I used to think they made the journey from the soil to the surface of the snow but careful digging showed no sign of them. I have since read they live in bark cracks on tree-trunks and branches while the ground is frozen; presumably they constitute a large proportion of the food that the nuthatches and chickadees extract as they flit about the trees. A couple of really warm days, at any time of the winter, is enough to bring the snowfleas onto the surface of the snow in their millions where the topography of the snow surface concentrates them in hollows such as footprints. Once in a while they hit a puddle. They are so tiny they can float on the water where they resemble a coarse powder the colour of iron filings. What stimulates them to advertise their presence in this way? Is it a mating ritual? A sort of bouncing macho dance?

Of moose and deer around my cabin in winter, there are no signs. Caribou tracks occur occasionally but these animals are either lower down in the forest or up above timberline on the windswept ridges where their winter food, lichens, is available to them. Goats also find sustenance on south-facing cliff ledges where snow is blown free.

It is generally assumed that ungulate meat forms a normal part of the diet for a wilderness dweller. While I don't doubt that for many that is the case, I have never killed anything larger than a rabbit. The main reason I don't pursue larger animals is, I suppose, laziness. Firstly, I would have to buy a rifle (I would have to be an extremely good stalker to get anywhere with a shotgun), then practise with it (which I would not enjoy), stalk the moose and kill it, and finally pack it home which, because the nearest place where moose are likely to be seen is several miles to the east and at a much lower elevation, would involve a very long haul. When you consider the time involved and the cost of the weapon, tags, ammunition and wilderness transportation, it is actually cheaper to buy meat. (Contrary to popular belief, all recreational hunters have meat transportation securely organised, be it a horse, truck or plane. Horses and planes are available to but a few and while that might seem unfair to those who don't have the money for these expensive conveyances, if these are the only vehicles available, the wilderness is unlikely to be overhunted.)

Were I infused with an enjoyment of the kill, I would probably not find hunting chores onerous. Unlike Isak Dinesen, a gun is the last thing I need either to prove myself or to rationalize my presence in the wild. If rabbits and grouse were plentiful, I would trap them but they are not, so I leave them alone. But in between leaving the Atnarko and taking up this claim, I wintered in a friend's cabin south of Kleena Kleene, a little farther towards Williams Lake. That cabin was a mere ten miles from the highway and an old logging road took me three quarters of the way there. (Logging roads swarm all over that country now for most of it has since been clearcut.)

But there, in the scrub-birch swamps and thickets of spruce about the cabin, before the machines laid all to waste, rabbits abounded. The only human neighbour I had that winter was a native trapper who was camping about four miles away in a little shack too small to stand up in, and who used to pop in once in a while for tea. After one visit, he left me a roll of snare wire.

I set the thin gold loops as the trapper had shown me, in a patch of brush where rabbits' feet had made regular trails among the spruce roots and red willow bushes. I indicated the sites with survey ribbon gleaned from trees that had been marked by hunters in the fall but who never cleared up their plastic. When I returned the next day, skiing through the forest then wading knee-deep through the loose snow where I had strung the snares, I found a rabbit in one of them. It was surprisingly small. Its fur was white on the surface, but the soft down underneath was grey and tawny: rabbit-coloured.

A death is always saddening and yet there was almost a rightness to the light and stiffening body I held in my hands. I had lived in the wilderness for years but only as an observer; this was the first time I had deliberately planned a wild creature's death. By initiating my own killing I was conscious of becoming involved with the wilderness in a way I had never been before.

I'd had some experience at skinning animals but that had been mostly on farms. The rabbit was different; its body was tiny and its covering papery thin. I cut the back legs free then eased the skin over the animal's head like pulling off a sweater. But although I worked as carefully as I could, it was clumsily done and I ripped it in two places. I split a section of wood from a stove length and shaped the end so that I could stretch the skin over it, fur side in; I hung it on a nail under the porch to dry. Another, and I would have enough to line a pair of gloves.

That night I dined off rabbit stew. It had a delicate flavour but the lean, dark meat had to be eaten with care for the small, brittle bones snapped like matchsticks. It is amazing that this harsh and unforgiving environment should create such a thin-skinned, easily-broken animal.

When I went outside to toss the stripped bones to the eager dog, the night was very dark for the moon was past the full and had not yet risen. The sky was clear and choked with billions of stars, glimmering and quivering in the spaces between the trees and over the frozen lake. I touched the rabbit skin where it hung against the cabin wall. It had stiffened and hardened in the cold, but the fur that sprang from around the edges was cool and sensuous with a life of its own. It was weightless beneath my fingers, slippery as silk and soft as snow; faintly pale and mysterious, and magical in the starlight.

# chapter 14

## *spring*

*... When our human methods of transport are so perfect that physical laws no longer regulate our journeys ... that delightful feeling of oneness with (nature) will have gone from our wanderings forever.*

Freya Stark, *The Southern Gates of Arabia*

Spring rushes on apace and with it the time left for me before I must go out once more to earn some cash. In the seven years I have been at Nuk Tessli, I have yet to see the transition from winter to summer. Even though I have quit tree-planting, art shows, slide shows and print-making workshops occupy these months and I still must leave home in late March or early April. At Nimpo the ice is beginning to go and soon no one will be able to fly. Conditions underfoot will become increasingly difficult; no matter how scattered through the calendar my spring bids for income might be, once I leave here it will be many weeks before I return.

Spring means that the chimneys must be swept. In winter they need very little attention for the big barrel heater has a straight flue that stays free of soot. But I do it anyway before I go away for it is easier to get onto the roof when snow still lies to the eaves. I drag the ladder around first thing in the morning while the snow is firm, but do the sweeping when the day has warmed and I can let the stove go out and the chimney cool. The ladder is then removed back to its storage place behind the woodshed for, if it were left in place, the thin metal roof above the attic would provide little challenge for a breakfast-hungry bear.

It is fortunate that the poorer light of the darker months hides the accumulated grime in a cabin as much of it cannot easily be removed during the colder part of the year. Liquid on the outside of the windows freezes and that on the floor takes too long to dry and may even freeze there as well. So the day that these two items can be scrubbed is a landmark in the turning of the seasons. More of the floor is now freed of clutter; a lot of things, like the bucket in which the laundry soaks, can be put outside, as can poor old Lonesome, who is banished from her winter nest by the boots and coats and condemned, somewhat reluctantly, to one of the two dog boxes on the porch.

Spring means that washing not only does not freeze when hung outside, but on occasion it even completely dries. Spring means that instead of worrying if my meagre supply of kerosene is going to last, suddenly I am barely using the lamps and have a suprising amount of fuel left. Spring means pulling everything out of the root cellar beneath my floor and discarding all the mouse-eaten and rotten potatoes and onions; there will be a few good ones to re-inter when I depart from here but most of the fresh stuff will have been consumed. It is not likely to get supremely cold any more, but the temperature will still drop below freezing for quite a while and all cans and jars will have to be incarcerated in the hole while I am away.

The solar panels can be brought in from the ice and put in their customary summer niche on the deck. The batteries must be fully charged and the circuit disconnected before I leave. One of the canoes is dug out, lowered from the tree, and hauled across the lake to the end of the summer hiking trail. There is no easy way to walk around the lake from where the summer trail meets the shore and the canoe will be waiting for me when I return in June.

The usual inventory of food, computer and art supplies must be taken and I write long lists under the headings of each town that I will visit; what I will have to take with me, the things I will buy, and the people I will endeavour to phone, or fax, or see. (The fact that I will invariably lose these lists is irrelevant.)

But spring is by no means all work and worry. How wonderful it is to stride freely down to the lake wearing nothing on my feet but boots, for the snow has now settled into the overflow and frozen as smoothly as a sidewalk. How exciting it is to see small patches of bare ground appear beneath the trees and imagine, among the dead whips of vegetation, the plants that will soon be growing there. How enticing it is to smell the sun-warmed lichens on the rocks. A favourite walk at this time is to go to the outlet across the lake where an exhalation of warmth has opened a hole at the edge of the lake the size of a house lot. While travelling in the Middle East years ago I was struck by how exceptionally beautiful water looked in a desert. It is the same here after months of ice and snow; the sound and movement of water, the golden stones among the sun flickers on the bottom, the wind-furred ripples, the reflections: all take on an extra exquisite radiance never seen in the green of summer. The warmth has bared a chunk of river bank a whole four paces long. The dogs chew urgently at desiccated straws among the dull, winter olive of heather and Labrador tea, and there is the half-forgotten clash of the wind in the dead grasses.

Spring means the swamps are softening at lower elevations and the journey down the river becomes heavy and tedious. I stuck to its wearisome safety for a year or two after my brush with the November blizzard, but terrors fade with time and treks up the mountains behind the cabin had shown me that, in late March, the snow above the tree line is usually wind-packed and firm. It was not long before Horsetrail Pass beckoned once again. There were many more daylight hours to make use of, and given appropriate weather this would be a fabulous trip.

My first appointment outside that year was a slide show in Banff on April 10. I would need a minimum of three days' for hiking, two for driving, an extra one for emergencies, and two additional days at Nimpo to catch up on mail and reorientate myself into the outside world. I would have to leave on the third of the month at the latest.

The sun was usually warm enough to make surface snow soggy and sticky during the day, but at night it froze. It so turned out that the full moon was on the second; night travel, therefore, would seem to be the way to go.

To trek downriver to Sam's cabin then walk up to Fish Lake as I had done for the November trip was now not the best choice of routes. Forest snow was softer than that in the open and it would be easier to take the longer alpine hike round by the bridge. Nonetheless, the first section of the trail as it leaves my lake is steep and quite thickly treed. Even by the light of the moon, it would be shaded and quite difficult to travel at night. Several days before I wanted to leave, I slogged to the top of the ridge and back on a warm afternoon in the hopes that it would be firm enough to bear my weight without snowshoes when I was packing all my gear. People think that, because I have dogs, I should be able to hitch them to the toboggan and ride all the way like a queen. But sled dogs can work effectively only in comparatively flat, open country with trails broken out for them. Even if I used the dogs on the lakes, I would still have to drag the sled myself up and down through the forest—either that or spend countless hours extricating it and the dogs from bush and windfalls. And I would have to tramp down the trail in front of them when the snow was soft. So I find it easier, in this mountainous country, to give the dogs packs and carry a few extra items like sleeping bag, down coat and camera (none of which I would trust on a dog in any case). Added to this is the axe and, when I don't need them, the snowshoes. The clothing and camera are stuffed into a backpack and the straps of this are arranged so that, when the terrain is steep and the task of hauling even this light load becomes a trial, the whole lot can be slung on my shoulders, toboggan and all. For me, this seems to be the best way to make use of my energy resources. If the blue, plastic carapace gives me the look of a displaced beetle, the dogs seem to accept it as just one more weird thing about this peculiar human with whom it is their lot to be involved.

To take advantage of the frost, I was across the lake well before sunrise, but I did not expect to travel very far on that first day. At the top the country levels out and remains fairly flat for about four miles. But there, golden fingers of sunlight had already poked through the trees and a warm, southwest wind was blowing. At once the surface snow became sticky and progress was a massive-footed slog.

Not far from the bridge, however, is a cabin—little more than a hovel, really—cobbled together by a long-gone trapper. Bob and Francie maintain it as an emergency shelter and, despite the early hour of the day, this is where I planned to wait until the frost tightened up the snow again. The cabin was pretty much buried in a large drift and I had brought along a shovel, which I would leave there and pick up again in summer, to dig out both the door and the chimney. This last had been completely flattened by the snow; there was not a trace of it. But by lining up the little tin stove inside with the two tiny, bear-spiked window holes and the child-sized, ill-fitting door, I could make a guess as to which part of the six-foot-deep mound on the roof I should excavate.

It had been two or three years since the trappers had passed this way and the little windows had long since lost whatever plastic covering they might have once possessed. Snow had blown freely through the holes and a huge drift occupied most of the tent-sized interior; I dug enough of this away to move past a tiny, warped stove and give me room to sleep on the floor, but otherwise I let it be. The southwest wind was warm and spring-like and I spent most of the day dodging tree shadows, sitting in the sun with a book. I kept a sharp eye on the weather, for it had been a southwest storm which had caused the blizzard over Horsetrail Pass before; if the weather deteriorated I would have to retreat back down to my cabin and go out along the river.

With only a couple of inches of candle to last me through the trip, I did not waste it in illuminating the darkness, but stretched out early on the dirt floor between the snowdrift and the wall. I never carry a watch but I have a good sense of time and can make myself wake up when I want to; by the moon, it must have been about one or two in the morning when consciousness returned. Rags of clouds still flew from the southwest but the sky was mostly clear and the moon was brilliant. There was just enough frost to tighten up the snow; a quick breakfast, and I was away.

Even here, where the forest was much more open than around home, it was suprising how tree shadows obfuscated the route. The snowshoes sank more than I had hoped, but remained gratifyingly

free of gumbo. I crossed Round Lake and climbed slowly but steadily through more of the open forest. Finally I broke free of the trees, and a brilliant, silver and indigo, whipped-cream world was spread about me.

The moon's platinum disc had enlarged and dipped appreciably towards the mountains. A few whiffs of cloud hung about the peaks and behind them was a darker wall of heaving vapour from which the flying rags of cloud were spawned. In the path of the moon, billows of snow evinced a thin glazing of ice which took on a mercurial sheen. The wind sang but, at ground level, although it was steady, it was not excessive. In a straggle of balsam I crouched to pull on extra garments and munch at a handful of nuts.

The first height of land marks the summit of a wide plateau that in spring is criss-crossed with a thousand snow-melt streams and in summer is a riot of flowers. No bare ground now, though, not even a rock. Just the moon-smooth blanket of snow.

The country drops a little over the next two or three miles and although the slope is gradual, the character of the snow changed at once. Because it was no longer exposed to the southwest sun and wind, it was looser and softer; occasionally it settled with a loud WHOOOOOF! This was invariably followed by an extremely soft band of snow a few paces farther on. Even with this telltale noise, however, these traps were impossible to detect. As much as I tried to anticipate them I was always caught unawares—the snowshoes would crash down, their toes would lodge under the crust, and I generally ended up on my face.

*Chris Czajkowski*

The slowly rising ground behind me temporarily hid the western mountains and the moon was now hanging very close to the horizon. The snow underfoot and my feet themselves were in shadow, but the thin, wind-driven layer that hissed loosely over the surface was still illuminated. It sped around my ankles like a streaming river, a singing, silver cloud of spindrift snow.

A full moon set as the sun rose and, as I approached the bend in the high valley which would take me to Fish Lake, the first glow of dawn appeared beyond it. I was travelling in full shadow now, but the peaks still glittered as in a dream. It always amuses me to try and mark the moment when daylight becomes stronger than whatever illuminates the night, but it is a subtle transition and difficult to pinpoint. All at once the eastern sky was greenish, then orange, and suddenly it was day. By the time the sun had climbed over the mountain I had reached Fish Lake and the start of the final climb to Horsetrail Pass. The weather looked promising but I would have preferred to keep going just to make sure, however after about six hours' travelling I was immensely hungry and not a little tired. A second breakfast seemed like a very good idea.

I collected brush and built a little fire on a mat of balsam evergreens which kept the initial flame from being quenched. I rammed snow into the billy then, when it melted, packed more in again, and soon had a good feed of tea and oats beneath my belt. The fire quickly melted into the snow and drowned but by then it was no longer needed and I was ready to scatter the ashes and go.

The break had been taken in a sheltered hollow and, as I pulled free, it became evident that the wall of cloud behind the main divide was spreading. The mountains in the west had dulled and softened at the edges. I had known summer storms to cross the intervening thirty miles in less than an hour so, although the sun burned nicely now upon my breakfast spot, it was not without some trepidation that I began to climb.

But what a contrast to that other journey. It was too damned hot! Even after I had stripped down to shirtsleeves, the sweat rolled off me. The heat at once softened the surface snow but, because the slope had been well burnished by wind and sun all throughout the winter, it was firm underneath and not sticky. Although the clouds still raced from the west, the wind at ground level had dropped and, every few yards, when I paused to allow the aches to leave my muscles, the hot, snow-glaring silence was supreme.

The last of the trees fell away and suddenly I recognized where I was. There lay the same pattern of rocks that I had dimly seen in the furious storm when I thought I had reached the summit. I could see at once where I had gone wrong. I had, indeed, been very close to the top of the pass, but from this rise the land dipped a little before climbing to the main ridge itself. I could see the gully that had enticed me back down to Fish Lake: if I had headed a merest fraction of a degree to the left, I might have made it over the pass after all. It couldn't be more than a quarter of a mile farther on. But, then, that short space, so gentle in this windless sunlight, would have been unimaginable hell in that hurricane; perhaps turning back was the best thing I could have done.

There was another surprise to greet me from this vantage point. The main ridge was bare to the bone. Where I stood, the snow depth must have been at least six feet (and would have been considerably more in leeward hollows) but the furious winds had swept the whole main ridge completely clean.

A quick glance behind me: the main divide had disappeared. The grey pall had travelled halfway across the sky. But I would make it now. Over the top, no weather in the world could hurt me.

There is a delicious moment before one reaches a summit. Instead of another rise, the peaks that come into view are the distant ones on the far side of the new vista. Tiredness forgotten, every step brings an increasing feeling of space until suddenly the land before you no longer climbs but swoops and leaps and slides into the new world.

How dark the snowless hillside looked; how strange to feel and smell rock and soft, squishy earth beneath my feet. Far below was the chain of small lakes that lay like beads down Maydoe Creek. On the far side ran the summer hiking trail. Where the valley widened, the broad, greyish streak of Charlotte Lake sprawled; into the blue distance beyond spread the wide, rolling Chilcotin Plateau, patchworked with clearcuts, most of them already brown and clear of snow. Even the sky was different over the Chilcotin. Level lands are surmounted by piled, flat-bottomed clouds which are very unlike those that twist about the mountains.

Although any route north at this point would have taken me to Nimpo eventually, the best one to take required some thought. The binoculars revealed a network of open leads and confirmed the rottenness of the ice on Charlotte Lake; crossing it and going out on the more direct road was therefore not feasible. This meant I would have to angle to the ranch where I left the truck in summer. There were no caretakers that winter—they come and go like autumn leaves—and my truck was not there either so I would have the extra fifteen-mile hike to the highway to look forward to.

The problem was how to reach the ranch. I had three choices: I could stay on the bare, rocky side of the ridge; attempt the more snowy, sheltered side while still keeping high; or descend to the bottom of the valley and travel down Maydoe Creek. There, I could use the ice if it were good (unlike Charlotte Lake, these ponds still looked solid and white) or connect with the summer trail if it were not. The trouble was that, somewhere in the descent, I would hit deep, rotten snow. From this altitude there appeared to be no bare ground between the trees along Maydoe Creek; if the snow was deep there, trekking along the trail would be very hard work. It would, in that case, be expedient to stay above the tree line for as long as possible.

All at once, the sun disappeared and a surprisingly chilly wind sprang up. Ahead, the Chilcotin still gleamed in soft-patched sunshine but behind me fingers of vapour were streaking swiftly overhead from the west.

The rocky side of the ridge seemed the best bet for a while but it would soon become very rough and would eventually take me too far out of my way. About a mile east there was another dip in the ridge; I could keep on the rocks for now and make a decision then. I pulled on clothes against the chill, scooped a couple of handfuls of water from a trickle below a snowslab, hoisted my gear upon my back and started over the stones.

On the lee side of the second pass I came face to face with three bull caribou. Caribou have two obvious characteristics; one is to be constantly on the move, the other is an intense curiosity. This trio behaved in a classic manner. They ran away a few paces, stopped, and ran back again. On a caribou the bit of leg that horse people call a pastern is extremely long. This gives the animals a pronounced, springy trot, a pace no doubt well suited to their environment but one which looks both exaggerated and affected. The group pranced back and forth several times, posing beautifully for my camera amid the rocks and streaks of snow.

If the snowshoeing had been good, I would have continued to stay above the tree line for a while, but on the far side of the ridge the snow was not well packed. Daylight would fail soon and the weather continued to look threatening so I plunged down into the forest. The instant I hit trees, I sank to my knees, snowshoes and all, at every step.

The priority now was simply to lose altitude in the hopes that the going would improve. However, the slope was not steep and progress continued to be slow for some time. After a while I found myself beside a small, snow-roofed creek in which running water could be heard. The light was going and I made camp by a hole where the roof had collapsed into the creek and I could fish water out by tying a billy can to a long string. The tarp was rigged in anticipation of the rain I was sure would come. However, despite a heavy overcast, the night stayed dry. Unfortunately, this also meant that here was no frost and the deep-snow struggle was at first no better in the morning.

The depth finally decreased quite suddenly and significantly at the bottom of the valley. Despite their unflawed surface from a distance, the chain of little lakes was not worth risking and I got wet feet crossing the creek. But the summer trail provided a suprisingly good surface for on it, under the trees, the snow was compact and icy. The country was fairly level for a while but I was entering a drier climate by the mile and soon hit patches of bare ground. For the last hour and a half, the trail dropped steeply again. It followed the edge of a little canyon and was exposed to the sun. Bare ground predominated and finally took over, and that, for me, was the end of the snow.

Bob and Francie use a cabin at the ranch as a base and in it I stacked the toboggan, axe and snowshoes. I would pick them up when I came back with a vehicle in summer. With no caretakers in residence, there was no point in detouring to the main house. I managed about half the forestry road before the day's end. The promised storm had simply been bluster and it had retreated from whence it had come, leaving the sky cloudless again. The last of the sun painted the trees orange with the low light of the flatlands and the snow-covered mountains I had so recently left were now no more than a distant, flaming banner crimped tight against the horizon.

The Chilcotin is little more than a desert in ecological terms and, without snow to provide water, camp sites are few. I made for a large slough and found it completely ice-free and brimming with water and ducks. Pussy willows sported their furry pelts around the edge. And, now that I didn't need it, there was a good, hard frost. My snow- and sweat-sodden feltpacks were rigid as iron and had to be thawed before I could jam my feet into them in the morning. But summer was not far away. Around my head as the sun went down flew a lone and hopeful, yet sadly disappointed mosquito.

chapter 15

# bear facts #3

*... Male black bears range through overlapping areas covering about 200 square kilometers each in the mountains ... Bears have good memories (for food sources).*

Ben Gadd, *Handbook of the Canadian Rockies*

Two years after his first efforts, Gold Tip broke into the cabin again. At least, I assumed it was him, for the MO was the same. The intervening summer had been uneventful, at least as far as bears were concerned; I had seen no sign of Gold Tip since Sport had treed him and had hoped he had retired to greener pastures, if not in this world, then in the next.

I was very late back from spring work that year—July had already begun. The news of the break-in was waiting for me at Mary's resort for, with the ice long gone, Nick Christiansen had flown to the cabin, taking a friend to see it, and brought back the news: "There's glass all over the place and one helluva mess." So as I slid open the home-made bolt on the door (still bearing the gouge from the first attempt at entry), I was not altogether unprepared for what I would find.

Since the original break-ins, the small panes and wooden divisions of the previously broken windows had been replaced with single sheets of glass. The old fashioned medians had looked attractive from the outside of the cabin but, from inside, the uncluttered panes were vastly superior. I liked the improved view and extra light so well I had traded these two windows with ones that looked onto the lake. Thus when the bear climbed onto his rock, he was once more faced with divided panes, and the glass fragments, wood slivers and chunks of old putty were piled on either side of the sill. I had not left the shotgun trap set for fear some other agent might set it off in my long absence.

The inside of the cabin was blessed with the inevitable chaos but there was, in fact, very little damage. Rugs had been kicked aside but the boards over the root-cellar had not even been removed; a few books and utensils had been batted about but nothing was seriously clawed or chewed; the batteries had been left alone. It was as though the bear was not really all that interested in taking the place apart, but, having made the effort to get in, felt he had to toss a few things around to make sure that I knew he had been by. Even the table, resurrected since the last debacle, had remained solidly on its feet. I had, however, not left this under the boulder window as had been the case before, but had removed it to a position beneath the other west window. The bear, although he could have climbed with very little effort from the floor to the sill beside the boulder, found the table far more convenient for his purpose and therefore the window above it an easier way to exit. Thus I had two broken windows instead of one. From the breakage pattern, it looked very much as though the shutter had still been up when he went out. But the bear was an old hand at windows by this stage and they no longer held any mysteries for him. He had burst through with such determination that not only the divisions but the frame, the shutter, and its seating were little more than kindling.

There would be the repairs and clean-up to do, and plastic and screens to put over the holes, but I was like a kid out of school with the summer before me and little could depress me at that stage. The day was bright and the bugs were hardly noticeable at that point so there was no great urgency for anything; first I did what I always do when I arrive home—lit the fire, hauled water and made tea.

There was quite a lot of debris inside which puzzled me a little at first without thinking very much about it. A few leaves of dead grass, blown needles and a couple of odd bits of dried mud littered the floor. But there was a feel about the place as though the break-in had not been very recent. There was a permanence about the mess, a sort of comfortableness about the dead vegetation, as if the interior of the cabin had already begun the process of reverting to nature. There were also the remains of two rufous hummingbirds on the east windowsill. If any door or window of a dwelling is open, these birds inevitably zoom in. The two casualties would have immediately gone to the light and been unable to find their way back out. Ants had almost completely disposed of the carcasses; there was little left other than the needle beaks and wisps of ruby iridescence, for their gorgets were unaccountably intact. Their desiccated state indicated that the cabin had been open for two to three weeks, which would place the bear's visit in mid-June. This seemed very likely for it duplicated the timing of his first break-in and wild animals' yearly rounds are generally very regular.

As I drank tea and contemplated the vagaries of the universe, I became aware of a couple of barn swallows chatting companionably. Their burbling conversations are soothing and give the impression of a great devotion. How nice it would be to live without windows at

all, I mused. Those birds sound so close, they might almost be inside.

They were inside. They were sitting on a wire frame strung under the ceiling to support a drying rack above the stove. The gobs of dried mud suddenly made sense. I twisted my head behind me and on a high shelf of books above my bed was their nest.

Like the bear, the birds had literary inclinations. Securely supported by the toe of the shelf and sandwiched between T.S. Eliot and D.H. Lawrence, they had appropriately picked, for the centrepiece of their future brood's home, *Brave New World.*

The mud on the upper layers of the nest was not yet dry. What I would have done had there been young ones in there, I do not know. Fortunately there were not even any eggs. It wasn't the swallows so much that I minded—it might have been rather fun to have them in the house—but I could not see how I could give the parents access while keeping out the bugs. These would be a real pest both in the evening and on dull, humid days. So while the would-be parents chattered amicably outside, sitting on the rocks with white feathers for the lining of the nest in their beaks, I regretfully sealed their fate.

I felt a heel in more ways than one for this was the barn swallows' third attempt to use the cabin as a nesting site. All of them had failed. Tree swallows always live in the dead stump that gives Snag Island its name, but they never use the buildings for habitation. Bird books tell us that trees and rock-faces were the original barn swallow's choice but one wonders at their current propensity for human constructions, especially as, in western North America, it is only comparatively recently that buildings tall enough for them to use have been present at all. The trappers' shacks have never been tenanted in that way—presumably their eaves are too close to the ground for the birds to feel safe. The nearest building the size of mine is a considerable distance away.

The cabin stood for two summers before the barn swallows discovered it. During their first year, they gathered beakfuls of mud from the water's edge and tried to plaster it onto the front gable end of the cabin. But the sun shines full on that side and all the birds' efforts soon dried out and fell off. This was not surprising for the mud was not soil at all, just coarse-flaked, peaty duff; I did not see how such material would ever hang together well enough for a nest.

The second year, however, they stuck a compact little cup quite successfully to a beam in the porch roof right above the doorway. Eggs were laid but the birds did not seem to want to brood and no young ensued. Eventually the adults flew away and the eggs also disappeared.

The bookshelf with its solid support and wonderful protection from the weather (broken windows not withstanding) must have seemed a truly lucky find. When I turfed them out, the female must have been about to lay for, after a day of agitated flying and calling, she deposited some eggs in the previous year's nest on the porch. But it was obviously not to her liking. Within a day or two, fragments of eggshells freckled the ground and the project was abandoned.

At a lower altitude, the birds would have had the resources to start again, but up here the season is too short to allow a second attempt.

A year after Gold Tip's third break-in, the swallows (always assuming it was the same birds) finally produced a batch of young. They refurbished the old nest in the porch, putting a fresh layer of mud around the lip and lo and behold, four babies came into the world. They were absolutely stuffed in that nest for they had no more than half an inch of headroom. I was highly entertained by their antics and watched them shoving each other around in their incredibly tight quarters; they had to get their little bottoms over the edge to defecate, then elbow and heave and punch until somehow they managed to get their heads outward again. It seemed incredible that this could be done without one of them falling out. It always resulted in a change of order when this happened and, having read that the parents react only to size of gape when feeding nestlings, I wondered if all the babies would receive an equal share of food. Either the stimuli were much more subtle than I could see (which might well have been the case) or the parents knew exactly which baby was which, for I could determine no favouritism whatsoever. For me it was a bit like the infamous shell game where one tries to guess which cup the pea is under as the dealer shuffles them around. But the parent, flying in with a beak bristling with insect legs, would contemplate the brood for a moment and sometimes pick one right at the back who hardly seemed to have its mouth open at all. They were certainly behaving as if they could recognize their offspring as individuals.

Interestingly, although barn swallows are normally communal birds and often nest in close proximity to others of their species, should the tree swallows over on Snag Island come close to the cabin, there was always a lot of fuss. This was puzzling for neither group of birds was a threat to the other and their food was hardly in short supply.

The babies made an appalling mess right on my doorstep. I thought to hang a dog food bag below them to catch their offerings, but the parents were so upset at this innovation I was worried they were going to desert the nest. The bag was removed and tacked onto the step below. I had to remember to take an extra long stride every time I went out of the door.

I was not present when the babies launched themselves into the air as I was out guiding at the crucial time and when I came back the nest was empty. But the four young swallows wheeled confidently about the eaves and roosted in the porch for quite a while.

Year five of the swallow saga saw a new nest built on the side of the cabin under the eaves. I congratulated the parents on their far more convenient choice of site. Eggs were laid; the babies hatched; and I prepared to enjoy the entertainment once again. But the poor-quality mud did not adhere properly to the logs and, as the babies grew bigger, the nest fell to the ground. Three babies were already dead when it was discovered and the fourth looked in poor shape. I tacked a crude shelf right against where the nest had been and put it back in place. The parents accepted this readily enough, but the following morning I observed the mother looking speculatively into the nest, then hopping on top and waggling her body as if she was trying to brood, then getting off and looking inside again. As she flew away, I pulled the ladder round to look; that baby had succumbed as well. So in five years only one batch of youngsters has been successfully reared, and of those four offspring, the odds are long against even one of them surviving to return. The shelf and the old nest have been left in place and it is to be hoped that future efforts will be less traumatic.

As far as the bears are concerned, I have never knowingly seen Gold Tip again. Judging by the action of the dogs, there is generally a bear in the meadows close to the cabin in the spring, but in the years since the third break-in I have always managed to be back home in May or early June and if Gold Tip is in the vicinity, he keeps himself out of the way. Throughout the summer, the trap is set up every time I go for a hike, but it has never been triggered so I still can't be sure that it would work. Sure as fate, though, the one time I neglect to arm it, Gold Tip would be in.

In case this is beginning to sound as though I live constantly surrounded by salivating fangs and bloodstained claws, it should be remembered that the incidences in this book span a decade; some years I do not see a bear at all. But there was another bear incident of note. It involved an animal I first met while I was still building the cabins. I came to think of him as Ginger Bear.

I lived in a tent until the guest cabin was erected and had a couple of alarms with this bear around the camp. He batted pots about, attempted to get into my food crate, and tipped over a full, five-gallon gas can, thoughtfully holing it with his claws as he did so. When I finally managed to get a good look at this bear, he proved to be quite an unusual colour. His head and ears were jet black and short-coated, but his body fur was as long and luxuriantly red as that of a fox. He was not very big and had a gangly, teenage look so it was probable that he was not long parted from his mother.

A year or two later I had been away for a few nights on some trip or other and arrived home in the middle of the day by canoe. The weather was calm and blue and summery; Lonesome had ridden across the lake in the boat, and Sport had swum behind. The cabin was in order; I defused the trap and I went through the usual tea-making routine. Just as the water boiled, there was a crash of brush, a scratching of bark, and a cacophony from the dogs. I flew to the door. Right behind the outhouse was Ginger Bear.

No gawky teenager this, however. He was now a magnificent creature; his summer coat was rich and long and glowing like a flame. But he was behaving oddly. He did not run away but simply sat, and then lay on his stomach beside a rock in the hot sunshine. He did not seem particularly aggressive and did not approach the cabin, but neither would he leave. He was such an unusual colour I thought I would try for a photograph. Camera in one hand and loaded shotgun in the other (and a bunch of spare shells in my pocket), I took a few very cautious steps closer to where I had a better view. At once he sat up and looked very alert, staring hard in my direction. Should I shoot or what? Why did he not go away? I backed off, he lay down. I went towards him again; up flew his head and that intense gaze bored into me once more.

Obviously, we had reached a stalemate. In the end I thought I might as well have my tea and see what happened. As long as he stayed put the dogs were silent but they would warn me if he came too close to the cabin.

I actually forgot about him; the dogs snoozed and I became engrossed in a book. It must have been half an hour later when there was another furious crashing, scraping, and barking. Outside I went and there was Ginger Bear, hightailing it through the brush—with two coal black babies in tow. Ginger Bear was not a "he" at all; she was a mother. The babies must have been sitting up a tree until she deemed it safe for them to come down.

I saw Ginger Bear around once or twice during the next couple of years, and Bob mentioned she had been around his camps also. But then I did not see her for a while. One day, I happened to run into Dave and Rosemary Neads (my neighbours at The Precipice) in Anahim. "We've such a pretty bear in our meadow," said Rosemary. "She's quite red and she's got two black cubs. Look! I have a photo of her."

Sure enough, it was Ginger Bear.

# chapter 16

## *taya*

*These men wanted dogs, and the dogs they wanted were heavy dogs, with strong muscles by which to toil, and furry coats to protect them from the frost.*

Jack London, *Call of the Wild*

One summer morning, a strange, irregular slithering thumped along the boardwalk outside the cabin. It sounded a little odd but I put it down to some idiosyncrasy of the dogs and forgot about it.

Some time later, when I called the dogs for a hike, I was disturbed to see that Lonesome could barely walk. She seemed to have some kind of paralysis in her back legs. She did not appear to be in any pain, but her back half did not seem to be connected to her front half and it kept falling sideways, producing the stumbles and staggers I had heard before. We had been home several days from the last major hike (she sometimes walked a little stiffly after these—as did I) and I couldn't remember any recent fall she might have had; neither did there seem to be any broken bones or undue soreness or swelling. It was all quite mysterious.

There was little I could do about it. The nearest vet was at Williams Lake, a two-day walk and four hours' drive away. Tourists were due to arrive the following morning and, even if I radiophoned for a plane and flew to Nimpo, I could not have gone out to Williams Lake and returned in time to meet them. The dog was obviously distressed by her failure to function properly, but she was bright about the head and otherwise did not look sick; come suppertime she ate her food as usual.

Over the next ten days or so, she gradually returned to normal although her ability to negotiate the rocks along the waterfront never completely recovered and she often fell in while trying to get a drink from the lake. (Water in buckets was placed handy for her, but neither dog was used to such luxury and the lake was still her preference.)

I wondered how she would cope with a major backpacking trip. I had planned on botanizing the moraines at the foot of Mt. Monarch, the principal peak visible from the cabins. Although Monarch seems to raise his hoary head directly beyond my lake, his summit is in fact twenty-five miles distant and separated from my cabin by a spectacular north/south canyon four thousand feet deep. Directly west of the cabins, at the bottom of the canyon, is an almost flat watershed separating the ten-mile finger of Knot Lake, which runs south into the Klinaklini River, from the south fork of the Atnarko, which flows north. I had been across the Atnarko end of the watershed a decade previously because that was how I had first found my way to Nuk Tessli. The part I remembered was a horrendous swamp of truck-sized hummocks and water-filled hollows netted tightly with twenty-foot willows and alders, whose trunks sprouted horizontally as much as vertically. Forcing a way through it had been a nightmare.

Because Mt. Monarch is the highest peak in Tweedsmuir Park and, at twelve thousand feet is not much lower than Mount Waddington fifty miles south, it is attractive to climbers. The early summit-baggers had expressed their awe throughout the area with such romanticisms as Mt. Jezebel, Ogre Mountain and War Drum Glacier. (Monarch itself had obviously been named by a man—a small, insignificant tooth in front of it is called "The Queen.") Early exploration of the Coast Range involved a lot of heavy bush-bashing to reach even the base of these mountains, let alone climb them. Peak-baggers of today, however, can fly into Success Lake, at four thousand feet, right at the foot of Monarch itself. But the lake is too small to allow a loaded plane to take off, and all expeditions must walk down to Knot Lake to be picked up. If the climbers could walk down, I reasoned, I could walk up.

By the time I wanted to leave, Lonesome seemed much as usual. However, I didn't like to risk putting a pack on her and so Sport and I were the only ones carrying loads. And they were pretty hefty ones— not only were we packing for ten days, but we also had to carry Lonesome's share of gear and food between us. This does not sound much but it was surprising what a difference it made. I consoled myself that, for me at any rate, the monstrous pack would last only a day or two: by then we would have eaten some of the food and a lot of what I had left could fill up the gaps in Sport's load. Although his would stay much the same, mine would rapidly improve; he would not be aware of my subterfuge.

When I first came up from the Atnarko cabin to explore Nuk Tessli, luck had favoured me with a likely spur which proved to house a major game trail. From the bottom, the trail had been impossible to miss but, even when I had returned to the Atnarko a day or two after first coming to Nuk Tessli, connecting with the top of the spur had proved elusive and bluffed impasses twice forced me to laboriously climb back up again and cast around. After ten intervening years, I wondered how easily I would find it.

To my immense surprise (for I have no sense of direction whatsoever) I hit the top of the spur dead on. But either my physical abilities had deteriorated dramatically or my memory was playing false, for it seemed a much rougher trip than I recalled. I had certainly forgotten how far down it was; having plunged coastward through brushy undergrowth for many hours, I reached the bluff at the top of the spur, to discover that I still had a depressingly long way to go. It was absolutely windless and monstrously hot. The creek I was loosely following and which might have given some relief was either out of earshot or buried deep in a steep-walled gully.

The bluff provided the only viewpoint on the descent. From it fanned a dramatic view of the opposite mountains and the wildly careering waterspouts that graced their steep, forested flanks. More important, I could see a good slice of the watershed including, at the southern end, a crescent-moon slice of the startling turquoise water that constituted the upper tip of Knot Lake. The willow swamp I had crossed before was easy to spot by its lighter, looser greenery; the Knot Lake end of the watershed was covered with a dark-tipped mat of conifer which was probably fir. Only a small amount seemed mature, the rest was somewhat shorter, as if a fire had been through at one time. But fir spelled drier ground and that seemed the logical way to go. Through the pelt of conifers ran several dry river beds of naked rock spreading over a great boulder fan that issued from one of the two major streams running from Mount Monarch. In a fall deluge during the late 1930s, some kind of natural dam—a rock- or snowslide—must have blocked the creek higher up and then blown out. The resulting wall of water scoured cut banks sixty feet high along the watercourse and swept clear across the valley, mowing down everything in its path and earning itself the name of Pandemonium Creek. I hoped that, by following it up, I would reach the moraines.

The landmark which had brought me to the top of the spur was a stand of beetle-killed lodgepole pine. After ten years, few of these were still upright and the blow-down had produced a horrendous tangle of pick-up-sticks through which we had to crawl, wriggle, slide, and climb, often slithering down rock-faces I would not have believed that some of the ungulates could negotiate. But there were moose and deer tracks for all to see. Sport wailed every time he thought he might be stuck but, judging by the fresh-turned soil in every toe-hold between the fallen logs, this was still a major route for wildlife; it must have been the only way up or down for a dozen miles in either direction.

The lower part of the spur ran through open mature Douglas fir forest, and I finally gained access to the creek for a drink at the bottom. As expected, the middle of the watershed was drier, and it proved to be much easier to cross than the willow swamp. As the ground rose slightly, one of the dry-stone riverbeds presented itself and led me to the point where Pandemonium Creek spewed from its cut banks.

It had been a dry summer and I had imagined that Pandemonium Creek would be easy to cross, but the water was ice-fed, swollen and roaring. Struggling along its tremendous, loose-cut banks, I was repeatedly repelled by bluffs. I spent two exhausting days trying to find a way up the creek. At the end of them I figured I might have a route, but still could not be sure what was around the next corner, and by then I no longer had the reserves of energy left to see. After the first side proved too difficult, I followed the creek down through the boulder fan, where it spread out into many skeins, in the hopes that I would find a less violent stretch to cross, but the swiftness and deepness of the silt-grey channels continued to defeat me and I was forced farther and farther towards the lake. That boulder fan rated among the roughest country through which I have ever had the pleasure of attempting to force a way. The willow swamp at the far end of the watershed seemed a highway by comparison. The dark, coniferous forest was fir all right, but as a result of Pandemonium Creek's exertions, the trees were not a great deal higher than my head and as dense as an unpruned raspberry patch. A lot of my journey was spent on hands and knees, dragging my pack behind me. Occasional tiny silty bars glittering with mica and imprinted with very fresh grizzly tracks showed clear of the water that roared like grey soup beside me. Neither I nor a bear would hear the other approach due to the racket of water but fortunately there were no encounters. I pretty much gave up on the idea of crossing the creek at all but thought I might at least go and see Knot Lake. Quite likely there would be a beach at the head of the lake, and as the weather was still hot and dry and I had plenty of food, it would be a pleasant place to camp for a day or two.

As I had surmised, there was a beach, or a silt flat rather, at the head of Knot Lake. The only trouble was, it was under six inches of water. The whole valley, from one precipitous side to the other, was wall to wall water, even well back into the dense second growth through which I had struggled. I had been wading in the water itself, it seemed, forever, carrying Sport's monstrously heavy pack along with my own, for most of the channels were well above his head.

Large drift logs were grounded on the flats and some of these could be maneuvered to make a camp. An enormous one in situ and another smaller log dragged in front of it made a comfortable couch with a backrest; a third made a platform for my feet. A large flat cedar slab kept my little fire from drowning. Farther back there was one tiny bump of ground clear of the water and by judiciously cutting a few willow twigs there was just enough room for my sleeping bag.

It was finally possible to cross Pandemonium Creek. Further explorations showed there to be a much better camping spot closer to Monarch's buttresses. Pandemonium Creek, when it had smashed across the valley, had left intact a piece of old growth tucked tight against the mountain. Here fir and cedar towered and the brown, duffy forest floor beneath them supported very little vegetation. A few cut poles and log rounds indicated the area had been well used at one time although all the saw marks were well weathered. There had once been a homestead at the bottom end of Knot Lake and the inhabitants had travelled to and from the outside world via the Atnarko. However, although the campsite would have made a good shelter in bad weather, it was screened from the lake by a tight band of willows that hid the view and at that time I did not need it.

Monarch's moraines might have proved to be out of reach on that trip, but the journey was by no means a failure, for I had forgotten how grand the country was from this lower elevation. From the underwater beach, much of Monarch itself was hidden by the bluffs and forested shoulder of the canyon wall but other peaks sprouted farther along the lake, and the ice-green water and the reflections in it were extraordinary. A further straggle of old sawcuts behind the homesteader's camp revealed remnants of their trail. Traces of their route were visible, even through overgrown thickets of alders across the many arms of the creek, and this made the trip home much easier.

Throughout the whole journey, Lonesome enjoyed herself thoroughly and negotiated the windfall tangles with ease. Of the three of us, she arrived home by far the least fatigued. However, her packing days were over, and carrying her supplies as well as my own was going to defeat the whole point of having dogs in the first place, which was to ease my aging legs and not theirs. So when I went out in the fall and visited the friends who usually look after my animals when I visit the city, I left her there for good. She was fourteen at the time and ended her days a couple of years later, in doddering, but happy, senility.


Lonesome had packed only about eight pounds, but Sport regularly carried twenty. Visions of how much easier another large dog would make my life prompted me to put the word out among friends. Not far from Lonesome's retirement home lived a woman named Betty Frank.

Betty Frank is something of a legend in central British Columbia. Now in her sixties, she still has the figure of a twenty-year-old and is always elegantly dressed. But for most of her life she has been a guide/outfitter and trapper, and a sled dog breeder and racer. (There is a great deal more to Betty's notoriety than that but, as Betty herself says, the story of her life will have to wait until everyone concerned is dead.)

In a chance meeting, Betty mentioned that she was looking for good homes for two female sled dogs that were no longer useful to her. One was infertile and had become too slow for the sled; I forget why the other was being given away. I needed a dog who was good with people and the infertile female, according to the young guys who were helping Betty look after her animals at that time, was "a love."

Around the ramshackle house in which the woman and her entourage were living, dogs were stationed in every conceivable nook and cranny. Half-grown pups as fuzzy as teddy bears tumbled over themselves and dived rapturously for my boots, seriously impeding any forward motion; eight smaller pups at the stuffed-toy, eye-opening stage were still with their mother in a kennel; and, in the house (where Betty entertained me at ten in the morning, wearing peach-coloured silk pajamas, smoking incessantly, and constantly on the phone ) there was a further litter of pig-like new-borns.

Taya was outside with a dozen other adults, each shackled to a tree. At first sight, she looked anything but "a love." She was barking lustily and leaping up and down at the end of her heavy chain, a well-chewed hunk of an unidentifiable, frozen carcass on the snow before her. She was huge, black and hairy. Large white teeth and a red slavering maw glittered within the dark mask of her face. On top of her head, extraordinary, stick-up ears sported halos of fur, looking more like radar detectors than any part of normal canine anatomy. One of the nearby dogs had a horribly deformed foreleg which, Betty informed me, had been mangled in a fight.

The back of my truck was already full and Taya had to ride on the seat. She had the greatest difficulty in staying there; every time she tried to lie down, half of her body slid off. However, she seemed resigned to this perpetual discomfort and evinced no other symptom of distress, which was a relief, for Sport vomited copiously in a vehicle so was therefore always a nuisance to take anywhere.

It was the end of December. Mary's driveway at Nimpo was ploughed but my "town house" was snowed in. Having shopped for five months' worth of supplies there was a large amount of freight to move. I had never seen a dog in harness, but Betty had shown me a rig and I braided a temporary one out of bale string. Taya sat down promptly as she had been taught and allowed me to lift her great feet and push them through the loops of the harness. She looked somewhat puzzled throughout my various ministrations so I was obviously not doing things  quite the way to which she was used, but could she pull! I had to remember, though, that she was not a household pet; when I gave her a bit of turkey skin she nearly grabbed my hand as well. (She very quickly lost this trait once food competition was removed and is now very much a lady when treats are proffered.) In due course, all the freight had been organised; now all I had to do was get it, and the dogs, back home.

By that time I had already given up foot travel in the early part of winter and, at Nimpo, I had to wait for Floyd to put skids on his plane before I could leave. But on January 2, I engineered myself, the freight, and both dogs to the local airport. With the two large animals on board, there was room for little else but some of the more perishable vegetables, a feedsack full of frozen meat and a bag of dog food—essentials that would have to come in with me in case something untoward cropped up and Floyd could not make it back with the rest of the freight on the same day.

Dogs seem to treat planes just like a car. I wish I could do the same. I understand perfectly the physics of flight and I have infinite faith in Floyd's expertise. But something happens that I cannot control when I have to get into an aircraft: every nerve in my body is screaming at me not to do it. There are those who quote fantastic stories of how their lives were saved by some instinct taking over and preventing them from doing what their reason told them was perfectly acceptable. If I listened to my involuntary urgings, I should never get anywhere near a plane at all. People often comment that I must be brave to live out in the wilderness, but the bravest thing I ever do is climb into a plane. (When I later saw the invoice, Lora had written on it "Fright to Chris Lake." She could have meant either flight or freight: but then Lora herself does not like flying so she might have known perfectly well what she was writing.)

Taya showed her worth again by hauling the freight from the ice to the cabin. At home she no longer needed to be chained and proved very rapidly to be, indeed, "a love." She was immensely strong; she moved through loose snow like a tank. Even from a distance I could see her wake curving against her chest like a bow wave. As I caught sight of her out of the corner of my eye my heart gave a small lurch, for the programmed image in my mind was "bear." Especially after she had lain in her box on the porch at thirty below and emerged grizzled with frost.

Her one fault was that if she had something to interest her, she did not readily come when she was called. I believe this is typical of sled-dogs. Right at the beginning, this independence almost proved her undoing.

By the outlet of the lake is a pool which is frozen only during cold spells when it becomes covered with thin and insecure ice. Without pause, Taya ran onto it. I have yet to find a dog with real ice sense. I called her back but she went her own way, and in she fell. She managed to get her shoulders out and there she stuck. I could not reach her from my side of the pool and I ran in snowshoes with nightmarish slowness around the end of it. I concentrated on where I was putting my feet and lost sight of her, hearing her whining, and visualizing an empty black hole in the ice when I got there. But by the time I had arrived, she had heaved herself out unaided, her fur seal-sleek with cascading water. She had considerably less bulk when wet, but the water had not penetrated her underfur for when I buried my fingers into her coat, I could feel the thick, dry warmth underneath. It was twenty-five below and her outer fur froze instantly into a matted web of ice; it was testament to the efficiency of the underfur that, for two more days until the weather turned milder, the outer ice on her coat remained intact.

## chapter 17

*weather*

*Other than the weather, when was the last time you heard anything on the radio that affected the way you spent your day?*

Neil Postman, *Amusing Ourselves to Death*

Taya's advent presaged a wonderful January. It was cold, between fifteen and thirty below Celsius most of the time, but the sun shone brilliantly from a postcard-cobalt sky and the snow was so shallow and compact I had soon visited many locations that are often too difficult for me to reach until March. The orange-tinted light that occurs during the six weeks around the shortest day was so clear that the purple shadow of my breath was etched onto the delicate, powdery hoar frost spangling the snow. As the sun poked over the southeast ridge, vivid sundogs slashed rainbow colours down to the lake; as the sun climbed higher, the air was aglitter with microscopic frost particles. Ice crystals grew upon the surface of the snow and on moonlit nights fairy fire glimmered on their elaborate and multiple facets. Below the pool where Taya broke through, the water of the river roiled clear of the ice and, beyond the barrier of shark-tooth pinnacles that marks the start of the rapids, the world was magical. Ice palaces and canyons housed hidden ropes of water, green-fanged where ground-ice coated the rocks. Exhalations of frost smoke crystalised onto every twig and leaf hanging over the river; feathers of ice piled onto themselves until they hung in great trailing beards like swarms of crystal bees. Dark, dumpy little birds tenanted this bitterhearted fairyland. Dippers are relatives of the robin but they have evolved the extraordinary ability to search for insect larvae at the bottoms of sub-zero, swift-moving streams. Their feather coats have a penguin-like density and, like their southern cousins, dippers also use their wings to "fly" underwater. But our little residents have no webbed feet to assist them in their maneuvering; instead, their toes are elongated and used to grasp stones while they walk along the bottom. Without these aids, the extraordinary insulating powers of the dipper's coat would keep them bobbing on the surface like a cork.

Dippers also inhabited the river in front of my cabin down on the Atnarko. There, they used to sing, a remarkable clear, bold melody which sounds to human intellect like nothing less than a glorious nose-thumbing to the bitter winter elements. But it is really a nose-thumbing to their neighbours for they are simply defending their winter food territories. Up here they are silent. I never see more than two dippers every winter—one in the short stretch of open water above my lake and the other below it. Each territory is sufficient for only one bird; they are separated by two miles of lake and they never meet—thus they never sing.

The dipper might seem impervious to the vagaries of climate, but for me, weather is the single most important factor that governs my life. It affects the amount of ice I must chop, the quantity of wood I must carry and dictates whether or not I can drip the worst of the water from the washing outside on the line or need to bring the clothes indoors, stiff as cordwood, to soften and drain over buckets by the stove. In normal times, the floor is my fridge, but if it is very cold, everything that will be damaged by freezing must be lifted onto shelves, then moved down as the cabin warms again.

The weather determines where I take my exercise—the wind forces me into the forest, the sun lures me onto the ice. But if the sun is too strong, the snow there may be sticky and I am driven to the forest again.

The weather affects my moods and my physical well-being. Like the solar panels, my own energy level is a great deal higher when the sun shines. On bright days I accomplish twice as much while during long dull spells my limbs ache and I am aware of and conscientiously have to fight the traps of depression. But the slow rhythm of snowshoeing through the patient, winter forest invariably restores much of my equilibrium.

Many people claim to be unaffected by the weather, but I think it is mainly because they simply do not notice its designs and are so conditioned by education to think that all emotion stems from the cerebrum, that they never link what is happening outside their skins to the way they feel. I once read an article by a man who surveyed people in the concrete canyons of Chicago; he blindfolded the interviewees and asked them what the weather was doing. It was a sunny day, but no sun penetrated to street level and only one out of the twenty participants could tell him that the sky was blue.

The forecasting of weather has always intrigued me, and I have observed the relationship between folkloric predictions and actual events for many years. As a child, for instance, I heard that if the new moon holds water, a dry month will follow. It was certainly the case during Taya's first January here, but I am afraid that on the whole this, and the bulk of rural axioms, make poor weather vanes. The new moon's angle is related to its phase and the distance the observer is placed from the earth's equator. The full moon's association with a frost is noticed when the sky is clear, but it is the lack of clouds which causes the frost. Most people are totally unaware that the moon is full if it happens to be a cloudy week around that time. Animals and plants invariably react to the conditions which have just gone by, not ones that are about to come. If the humming birds leave early it is because the summer has been dry and therefore their food plants have finished; if the coat of a mink is thick it is because it is already cold and has no bearing as to what will happen in January. If cows are standing facing one way under a tree it is either to catch a cool breeze, or stick their tails collectively towards a storm—or perhaps because they are looking towards the barn wondering whether or not it is time to be fed. (Ten years spent milking cows on commercial dairy farms gave me plenty of time to observe them.)

There are a few things that work. I remember an old fellow in England pointing out the swallows and telling me that, because they were flying higher, the rain was going to quit. And he was right. The swallows were following their food supply and when rain is imminent, bugs are low and biting. During high pressure, most of the flies stay a lot higher; sometimes, in the most stable weather, so far into the heavens that the swallows themselves are the merest specks as they wheel about after their prey.

In many places where I have lived, I learned to read local cloud patterns and predict the following day's weather from them quite well. But here, although my cabin has an open, sunny aspect, the narrow strip of sky along the horizon, which is the best weather guide of all, is hidden by the mountains. The most useful indicator here is the direction in which the wind is changing. If its point of origin swings more to the right, or clockwise, the weather is likely to become colder and clearer; if it veers to the left, one can expect warmer and usually more unstable conditions. If it happens slowly, the impact tends to be slight; if it happens quickly, the contrast can be dramatic.

Anticipating the direction of the wind change is sometimes possible. Cloud shapes and movements furnish clues, but I have often seen two or three separate layers of vapour, all flying in completely different directions at different altitudes above Nuk Tessli, while the ground wind bears no relationship to any of them. (This usually indicates instability—in other words, anything might happen.) When the January fine weather collapsed, it was slowly. Skeins of mares tails floated for days from the north, but they were combed from east to west indicating a clockwise change and it looked as though an Arctic front was on the way. Many of these fronts are preceded by some pretty nasty storms with unbelievably bitter winds that can last for days. This one, however, in keeping with the tradition of the gentle winter and slow collapse of the high pressure ridge, was almost apologetic. There was the merest mist of snow for a half a day then back to an aching, clear sky. But there was a slight difference in temperature. In twenty-four hours it had dropped twenty-five degrees.

That front was accompanied by an impressive display of northern lights. Greenish-white pulses shot towards me as rapidly as a strobe light, in horizontal sheets which I swear were below the level of the tree-tops.

Overnight I missed the signs of the wind veering back into the west; by the time I woke it had warmed right up and Nuk Tessli was beginning to sound in the trees. But neither front could quite defeat the other. Nuk Tessli, the warm west wind, lay over a layer of cold air poking up the valleys from the Interior, and the mix of the two airstreams brought the bulk of our winter's snow in February.


The weather regulates my computer time, and it also affects radio signals, both for the phone and the regular radio. I can receive broadcasts for the latter only during the dark hours and when there are no northern lights or falling snow between my cabin and Vancouver. On average, I pick up a forecast one morning in three, the crackling voices often fading in and out or mixing with advertisements and bits of a legal advice talk-back show from California.

It is handy to know the weather forecast, especially if a long overland trip is planned. When I first came here, the Vancouver CBC's broadcasts covered only the lower mainland and stopped short at Whistler, which is not only considerably to the south of me but is also on the coastal side of the mountains where the climate is vastly different. Vancouver is the only CBC station I can pick up and I wrote and asked them to extend the range of their broadcast, at least before 6:00 AM, after which I usually lost the signal anyway. I explained that there were a number of us in this radio-deficient area who relied on the weather for safety. We didn't expect information for our own locality, but if we knew what patterns were developing from the Yukon to Vancouver, we could make a good guess at what was going to happen. The 6:00 AM marine forecasts were not much help, because sea conditions bear surprisingly little relationship to what is happening on the Interior side of the mountains. Whether or not anyone else contacted the CBC with a similar request I don't know, but shortly afterwards, an extensive 5:30 AM weather report was instigated.

Apparently, there were many objections to this. The announcer would periodically explain that there were indeed other people who existed in the rest of the world and even in other parts of the province. But Vancouver people wanted Vancouver weather. They could not tolerate the loss of even five minutes out of twenty-four hours' listening time—and then only five days a week—for something that didn't directly concern what was in front of their noses.

During that winter, some skiers from the B.C. Mountaineering club rented a cabin. Two flew in with a load of food and the four others, under the leadership of Len Soet, skied in from the road. This event made history—it was the first time anyone had found there way to Nuk Tessli unaided and on foot.

It transpired that one of the skiers was, like myself, an early riser. He would pop over for coffee while the rest of his crew slumbered on. I was pleased to be able to give him a weather forecast and proudly told him of my possible part in his being able to receive it.

"It was YOU!" he snorted. "I can't stand that terrible start to the day. I get up and all I want is a relaxing cup of coffee and to be lightly entertained. I don't want to know what piddly bit of weather is happening in every whistlestop town in the province!"

The following morning, as soon as he saw me, he asked for the forecast. So I told him what was happening in Vancouver.

"But that's no good to me," he roared. "I want to know what is going on up here!"

The CBC, however, has succumbed to public pressure (no doubt called in from the non-climate of cars and buildings) and the forecast, while it does not quite stop at Whistler, has returned to a much skimpier sketch. But I don't really expect such services out here; I chose this life knowing that in a true emergency, my only resource is myself. And even if I have a province-wide picture of the weather patterns, I must still operate largely from guesswork. An Arctic front might travel down to Kamloops, but it might not come far enough west to reach me. Often, too, we have our heaviest snow when there is none forecast or received by anyone else, which is what happened during the Big Snow. All of that fell in a comparatively small, sparsely populated area and, had the woman and child not died, it would never have made the news at all. Whereas a couple of inches on the streets of Vancouver infuse the announcers' voices with the excitement of a world-shattering event. Which makes the rest of us laugh, but it is indeed a noteworthy occasion. It is one of the rare and wonderful instances when nature comes to town.

chapter 18

# a wilderness dogs dilemna

*There is no consensus among biologists as to why sex persists in spite of its obvious disadvantages.*

Adrian Forsyth, *A Natural History of Sex*

1996 was another big-snow year. At first the snow fell as a misty veil which only half obscured the mountains; the sun was visible for the most part, although it could be looked boldly in the eye. It was a period of comparative calm but interspersed by Nuk Tessli's playful gusts that flung dollops off the trees and thudded them onto the roof. Wind devils gyrated down the lake and whipped up tortured spirals of loose surface snow.

It was not until the first week in January that it began to snow in earnest. The overcast darkened and thickened, the sun disappeared and small, fast-falling flakes poured steadily and assiduously, rustling like taffeta as they tumbled through the trees. It was the kind of snow that meant business, the kind that was built to last. Six inches on top of the two-foot pack the first day, four inches at night, another two or three or six inches and so on. The days became a symphony of metallic greys; the nights amorphous and blank. Usually, in a snowless dark, the forested hills across the lake are sharp in outline, even on a cloudy night; now I looked out of the window, hooding my eyes against the flame of the lamp, and I could have been at the edge of an abyss; a capsule floating in a starless space. Daily I plodded over the trails through the bush to try and keep a couple of them open, wondering when the sun was going to reappear. But we had had this kind of snow before. It was still no precedent for what was to come.

The first summer that I spent here was graced by a ferocious windstorm. It was the main reason for the name Nuk Tessli—which is Carrier for "west wind." I was worried at the time that it might be a normal occurrence at this altitude and I was wondered how both my buildings and myself would survive repeated onslaughts of such magnitude. However, there has never been another storm quite so bad; the blizzard of January 1996, however, came close.

At noon, the sky was twilit. The winds screamed so maniacally down the lake that my nerves vibrated like guitar strings. So much snow was carried on the wind in addition to that which was falling that the world beyond the trees was obliterated, and to leave their shelter would have at once plunged me into a nightmare at least as bad as the blizzard on Horsetrail Pass. The air was so thick with snow it seemed as though one could cut it with a knife; its sheer weight was frightening. Sitting in the cabin I imagined the screaming drifts piling high and flowing over the roof on the uphill side of the building; outside, where the struggle of putting one clogged snowshoe in front of the other dissipated some of the claustrophobic gloom, it was hard to breathe.

Finally the wind died, but still it snowed. The small trees that were still visible were sculpted and bowed like gnomes. The larger ones drew the snow into them, droop-limbed, clutching it like a cloak. The world hung poised, waiting for a touch to free it from its burden. There is a washing line strung between two trees behind the cabin. In summer, I must stretch to reach it; as I am a tall person, the line would therefore be about seven and a half feet off the ground. The snow quit when it was six inches beneath it.

Once more I walked the trails, snowshoes muffled and swimming, webbing creaking, drowning in whiteness. Through the night the wind's soft fingers smoothed the counterpane of the lake and, apart from dimpled impressions close within the shelter of the cabin, it was as if I had never been.

That winter's snowpack had quite a few repercussions one way and another. It was followed by a very cold spring and a late summer. Tons of snow remained above the tree line all through the season and although the ice of the higher lakes broke into complicated plates threaded by cerulean and aquamarine canyons, a lot of them never completely thawed.

Gardeners at lower elevations were to tell me later that it was one of the worst years they have ever experienced. Everything was extremely late and many plants never flowered or fruited properly at all. The same thing occurred in the mountains, although the organisms which grow here are adapted to seasons of unproductivity and will simply lie dormant until conditions are more favourable. Normally, the timing of the flowers is amazingly predictable; each period of blooming pops up so regularly that I am able to schedule guided hikes around their appearance.

But that summer, clients who came at predicted times were disappointed, and others, who came later and who had not expected much in the way of flowers, were overwhelmed by one of the most spectacular displays it has ever been my privilege to see. I have hiked through many alpine meadows in different parts of the world but although some may have a more interesting or greater variety of species, few can beat North America for colour. Lupins are blue, the valerian is white, arnicas and senecios are yellow, mountain daisies are purple. But the principal species that dominates our meadows is the Indian paintbrush. There are many members of this genus and they evince all shades of red, orange, yellow, pink, purple and white, and occur from the Arctic to Mexico. But in these mountains, scarlet predominates. What is more, they are unique to the North American continent. They have a little-under-

stood semi-parasitic relationship with other vegetation and can neither be transplanted nor grown from seed. No other nation has a dominant red flower in its alpine ecology, hence our wonderful display. (Actually, the red part is not the flower. As with poinsettias, it is the leaves which turn colour. A close look at the plant will reveal a scattering of acid green horns erupting from trumpet-shaped, scarlet calyxes. These horns are highly adapted tubular flowers and with their brilliant red surroundings are nature-speak for: *Hummingbirds, come and get me.*)

Most years, when I first hike home in the spring, the forest is generally clear of snow and there are bare patches of ground through the alpine section. In 1996, the whole ten miles above tree line was under an unbroken white blanket. It was the second week of June, three weeks later than I'd managed to get home the year before. At Nimpo, Nick had told me he had flown over my lake a few days previously to find it also still solidly white.

About halfway between the road and the cabin, near Fish Lake, there is a creek which must be crossed; usually it is necessary to wade it early in the summer for the stones that can be used to step across are still submerged and won't be clear of the water for some time. But this time a precarious-looking snow bridge, barely thicker than a tree, was still in place. It was at a bad part of the creek—if I broke through I would be dashed down a small waterfall—but I thought I would give it a try. The dogs were told to stay and all three packs were laid on the bank. I had quantities of string with me and tied long lines to each pack. Clutching the strings, I pussy-footed across the bridge and hauled the packs over when I was safely on the other side. The effort involved seemed a little ridiculous in view of the fact that my legs and feet were already wet from the snow, but wading a swift, slippery-bottomed creek full of snow melt, in temperatures that are only just above freezing, is never very appealing.

Almost at the end of the alpine stretch is a wide plateau famed for its acres of lupins in late July. But now, only a few thin slabs of wind-blown tundra were sticking above the snow; the rest of the world was uniformly white. The weather had deteriorated; spits of sleety rain flew on a raw, sullen wind and the panorama of mountains I should have been able to see were hidden behind a wall of cloud.

All of a sudden Taya pricked up her radar detectors and stared intensely to one side; there stood fifteen caribou, all bulls, some last year's calves and only half grown and the others sporting huge, velvet-covered racks. Both dogs were enormously excited and, given half a chance, would have run after them. Taya was already on a lead as she will chase anything that moves if I don't restrict her, but I wanted to snap some pictures and I knew if I once took my eyes off Sport he would be gone, too. I needed both hands for the camera; there were no trees handy so I tied a dog to each leg. Although the caribou kept dancing away in apparent fright, they continued to circle round and come back in their usual ambivalent manner. But the sleet-sodden wind was creeping through the cracks of my clothes and it was too cold to hang about long. As I started to move again, the caribou ran off but moments later wheeled round in front of me once more where they trotted past in single file, silhouetted against a thick band of snow, the purple-black wall of cloud behind them. Suddenly, within three trotting heartbeats, the lead caribou dissolved. He didn't go behind anything, he simply paled and faded to nothing. Never breaking step, the second jogged behind and, within three paces, he, too, evaporated. The third and then the fourth one followed; heads up, evenly-spaced, all of them trotting steadily, one after the other, into grey oblivion. A photograph would have shown nothing; it was the movement that was so bewitching. The solid shapes, one by one, marching firmly, then simply dematerializing and vanishing. A *Star Wars* technician would have freaked. It was one of those unexpected and magical performances that nature obligingly tosses your way if you just happen to be there to see it.

The next moment, without warning, a solid wall of thick-flaked, falling snow swept over me and reduced visibility to no more than a few yards. This, then, was how the caribou had been so effectively eclipsed. I could only hope that I would not follow suit. The only directional indicator I had in all those miles of winter-bound tundra was the wind in my face. Fortunately it remained constant; equally fortunately I soon began to lose altitude and drop down among recognisable trees.

Progress had been very slow across the alpine for I had no snow-shoes and fell often into softened holes. Although this was the second day of my hike, I was still a long way from home. I camped just below the tree line, quite comfortable behind a thick, distorted pine that provided shelter from the wind. It was still raining and blowing somewhat the following morning; I had hoped for a frost to take me over the rest of the snow but it was not to be. Drifts lay in deep, soft patches in the forest but finally, on the last steep stretch down to my lake, the ground was mostly bare and I made better speed. Eventually I reached the water's edge, wondering if the water would be open for I was hoping for a plane load of freight the following day. There was no ice anywhere to be seen.

There was no canoe at the end of the trail, either. Normally one would have been dragged over the frozen lake during the winter but circumstances had made me go out earlier than was originally planned and hauling the canoe was one job that did not get done. No matter which way round the lake I chose to go to the cabin from there, I would be faced with a river crossing. I opted to go via the outlet. This was no longer the gentle stream that I often rock-hopped over dry-footed at the end of summer: the stepping stones, which span the river exactly at the point where the lake squeezes and tips smoothly into the rapids, were five feet under. And with the ice so recently gone from it, warm the water was not. The only alternative to wading was a thin, slim, fallen log that hung over a white-spumed waterfall quite a way downstream. The log looked rotten and the river was a dangerous maelstrom at that point.

I seriously thought about waiting until the following day when the supply plane was due; I should no doubt be able to signal Floyd to come across and pick me up. But if this weather persisted, no one would be flying and I might have to sit there for quite a while. (As it turned out, it was to be three days before a plane could come in.) I could see the cabin, for god's sake—I was wet, cold and tired and a night on the lake shore in these miserable conditions was not an at-tractive proposition.

I decided to risk the wade. I cached the packs and, before I had time to think about it too much, plunged in. It was still sleeting a little and I was dressed in full rain gear which was probably a mistake. Two steps and the current was fighting against my thighs. With the third, I was afloat.

Things seemed to happen slowly. Dreamily I bumped into rocks, tried to hold them, and felt my fingers lose their grip. Whitewater was only yards away. Fortunately the current was in my favour and it pushed me across the deep part of the river; a branch came within reach and I grabbed it—the rest was easy enough. I must have been in the water only a few seconds, but I remember every moment: the inexorable pull of water, the slow rasp of lichen-slick rock. Oddly enough, I never felt the cold. I am the world's worst procrastinator when it comes to getting into cold water for a voluntary swim, but whenever I have fallen in, even in the middle of winter, there is no temperature shock at all. I'm too busy thinking about how to get out. Not that I was very wet on this occasion for air trapped inside the raingear had kept me buoyant and the water had barely penetrated above my waist. But the raingear was no doubt the reason I had floated off in the first place

Within forty minutes, I was home. The wind dropped overnight and the sleet turned to snow so that when I took the canoe across the lake to fetch the packs in the morning, the ground was quite white.


As Betty Frank had told me, Taya was too heavy for deep snow. Even when I broke trail for her with snowshoes, she floundered like a landed fish. Thus I have not managed the long winter treks that I visualised with her. However, as a summer packdog, she is supreme. She carries thirty or forty pounds and although she gets excited at feeding time, she rarely barks otherwise except at bears, which suits me fine; there are few things that irritate me more than a uselessly barking dog.

Taya has a delightfully placid and amiable nature with humans and is adored by all visitors. But, I am afraid, small animals beware. She would be too slow to catch much in the normal scheme of things, but she has managed to grab more than just a couple of chickens on our trips outside. At home, given the chance, she will go for anything that moves, particularly deer, caribou and marmots. An uncontrollable dog in the wilderness is not only a nuisance, but has the potential to be very dangerous. If it sets up a bear and either chases it, or is chased back to its owner, there could be real trouble. We rarely encounter much in the way of animals in the forest (Sport had a run-in with a porcupine once; fortunately they are not common here), but above the tree line Taya has to be on a lead. A rope around her neck, however, does not mean "walk to heel" it means "pull." This is fine if we both want to go the same way, particularly uphill, but we have had definite differences of opinion when the marmots whistle. However, most of the time she stays with me well enough, and she and Sport between them pack such a lot of gear that for a four-day hike I carry nothing but camera, coat and sleeping bag; the dogs carry all the food, the cooking gear, spare clothes and the tent, and I can travel in unprecedented luxury.

There have been a couple of occasions, however, where Taya took off alone. Although she is infertile, she still comes on heat. My other dogs have all been male or spayed so I was not at first aware of the lengths to which a bitch will go when she wants to find a mate. Sport was fixed and although he showed a puzzled interest in Taya's condition, he was obviously not man enough to keep her home.

The first time Taya took off I was chainsawing, making lumber for an extension for the wharf. Lumbermaking is a hopelessly tedious and noisy job and for the couple of days I had so far been working on it, Taya had walked to the site then, when I started the mill, had come back to the cabin on her own. So I did not miss her until lunchtime, and then, when she was not around, hoped that she had simply gone for a short hike on her own which I did not encourage, but which she had done on one or two occasions. But when she still had not returned at suppertime, I radioed out to Mary at Nimpo and asked her to put notices in the stores. "Surely she wouldn't come all the way out here!" said Mary. Twenty-four hours later she turned up forty miles south of my cabin at Kleena Kleene where she had been spotted cavorting with a coyote. Mary's partner, Nick, was away so could not fly her back and I did not have time to walk out and fetch her. So I had to hire Floyd and a whole empty plane to bring her home; as she stepped out of the plane, she looked not in the least bit contrite.

In winter, if she comes in heat, the deep snow at the ends of our beaten paths defeats her. But when she started evincing signs of sexual excitement a year after her first disappearance, I watched her like a hawk. She was tied day and night and received a supervised hike each morning and evening. ("Just like a city dog," I would tell her, but she simply stared at me with her slanted eyes and a Mona Lisa smile.) At that time, a couple of young Australian women were renting the cabin. It was early fall; the underbrush leaves were turning, and frosts invigorated the mornings. It even snowed a little, only a few flakes with a skiff of white on the ground, but the Australians were so wondrously excited at something they had never seen before that I could not help but get caught up in their enthusiasm. I had just let Taya off for her morning run and was sufficiently distracted to forget about her for ten minutes—by which time she was gone. As before, I phoned out to Mary, but for several days there was no word. Apart from her value as a pack animal, I found I had grown fond of her and was surprised how much I missed her.

The nearest dogs that might encourage Taya to go gallivanting would be the wild ones—the wolves. Many stories are told about how dogs are lured among wolves and then killed by them. But if this happens (and a great many wildlife dramas are exaggerated) I don't think the wolves would deliberately entice a dog in order to do it in. Pack animals certainly communicate with each other to organise a hunt, but the human species is the only one which calculates vindictively. If dogs are torn apart by wolves I suspect it is because the domestic animal fails to respond correctly to the wolves' complicated hierarchical signals. At the other end of the scale, an equal number of stories claim part wolf ancestry for a considerable number of puppies; if that is the case, not all dog/wolf encounters can be unfriendly.

It had been quite a summer for wolves. On a couple of occasions I saw a single black one close to a small hill where I often camp with hikers. And when another party was with me later in the year, we climbed a high ridge looking for goats and received an extra bonus by being able to watch wolves chasing a bunch of caribou. Our observation point looked over a great tundra-like plateau and all the animals were a considerable distance away and difficult to see, even with binoculars. At first there appeared to be only five wolves but later we distinguished light-coloured ones which were so camouflaged

against the sandy eskers that they were all but invisible. Walt Disney was not directing the tableau so the wolves never got very close to their quarry and soon gave up and took a snooze. The caribou, which were probably a good mile ahead at that point, stopped and looked back a little uncertainly and quit running.

On the day after Taya's disappearance, I accompanied the two Australian women up to the last little shallow lake along my branch of the river. It nestles against the Tweedsmuir Park boundary and is an interesting bit of country, for years ago beaver dammed the creek. The dam has since gone out and it has left acres of black, peaty mudflats much frequented by wildlife. There are always a preponderance of animal tracks on these flats; that day they were frozen just hard enough to remain crisp. We found moose, deer, caribou and goose sign, and there was a plethora of wolf tracks. They were not in a business-like single file as I had seen them in the snow; it was evident that much jumping about and playing had been going on. Among the tracks were pawmarks half the size of the majority. They were slightly more oval, and might have been made by the rear feet of a young wolf, but they could equally as well have belonged to Taya. (Taya is undoubtedly as big as a wolf, but the wild animals' feet are much larger in proportion to their size.) The tracks stood out as boldly as print on a page, not only because they were partially frozen, but also because they had been made since the sprinkling of slushy snow had stopped early that morning. I called and called, both Taya's name and the best imitation I could make of a wolf's cry. But the only response was a small gust of wind on which dry snow flew; the woods stayed silent. Were the wolves listening? Sitting there still and soundless, slant eyes watching, among the rocks and wind-bent trees?

The Australians left and the bulk of a week went by. I had pretty much given up hope that I would ever see Taya again. But one evening a strange plane landed on the lake and there she was, looking over the pilot's shoulder from behind his seat. The pilot was a newcomer to the area who had just bought property on Charlotte Lake. He had flown up from the States that day and Taya had been by his cabin when he had arrived. I had scratched Mary's phone number with a nail on Taya's dog tag, he had found out who she was, and brought her straight to me. She had been gone six days and was very thin but seemed otherwise fine; no doubt she could write a good chapter for this book about her adventures if only she could talk. Lonesome took off twice in her wilderness career (because of bears, not assignations) and she was flown back as well. I seem to be destined to have neighbours all over the country flying my dogs back home from their wanderings.

# chapter 19

# another (shaggy) bear story

*Day 3*

*The plaintive cry of the loon will wake you in time for a hearty breakfast. Today our mode of transportation is small chartered floatplanes (6 pax. Beavers). Well provisioned with a picnic lunch, we take off from the mirrored surface of Nimpo Lake for an exhilarating day in the wilderness of Tweedsmuir Provincial Park ... We fly among the peaks of the Talchako Range and over the Monarch Icefields to view the glistening glaciers that constantly calve the icebergs drifting on the sparkling waters of Ape Lake. We land on Turner Lake, for the thrilling view of Hunlen Falls, which, with a sheer drop of 1,325 feet is one of Canada's highest. We also drop in for a visit with Chris Czajkowski ...*

Extract from an itinerary offered by
Leisure Island Tours, Victoria

At the start of that summer my finances were at a very low ebb. The previous craft-fair season only just made expenses; the spring work had been scrappy and, by the time I arrived at Nimpo prior to going home, the sum total of summer bookings numbered precisely one. I owed Avnorth for flights and Mary for rent and a host of other bills were rearing their ugly heads not very far beyond the horizon.

But at Nimpo, I received a message to contact Duncan Stewart of Tweedsmuir Air, another floatplane company based at Stewart's Lodge. Duncan asked me if I would like to accommodate some bus tours.

Bus tours?

For some years, a tour group had stayed two nights at Nimpo and spent the intervening day on an extensive flight-seeing tour. The rest of their schedule included a thrilling journey over the Monarch Icefield to the west of my cabins and a flyover, plus a hike, to Hunlen Falls. But they needed something else to round off their day. Would I be interested in giving them afternoon tea?

The largest number of people I had hitherto accommodated at one time at Nuk Tessli had been six—a full-sized bus holds forty. In previous years only one bus tour had been offered—this summer, because of the new ferry link between Bella Coola and the north of Vancouver Island, four of them had been booked.

The scale of the operation turned out to be by no means as formidable as might be supposed, at least at my end of it, for the tour group was divided into three parties which were staggered throughout the day, and Duncan's organisation was excellent. Three small planes—two Beavers and a Cessna 185 —were needed for each party. I was told to expect the first at 8:30 AM. There would be a changeover every three hours or so. On the first appointed morning, the tops of the mountains were socked in and it was drizzling; I wondered if they were going to arrive. It was with some bemusement that I heard the first plane come in low under the overcast, then watched it deftly paint a silver streak onto the mirror-calm sheet of water. Because islands and rocks surround the cabin, planes must land farther out onto the lake then turn and taxi through the obstacles. Passengers approach the wharf slowly and, from within their Plexiglas bubble, have plenty of time to appraise both the cabin and myself. But I stand there, smiling in welcome at nothing but the blank holes of windows. As the plane comes to the wharf, particularly the much larger Beaver, I must concentrate on catching the wing and easing it alongside a most artistic and beautiful snag. (All the pilots would dearly love to see the silvered, twisted trunk and tortured, lichen-splashed branches tidily in my woodshed; however, I like its weathered defiance too well to cut it down. A longer wharf would keep everyone happy, but one that projects into the water requires a separate lease that the insurance companies, in their wisdom, class as an airport and which, therefore, costs a great deal more than the land lease which houses the cabins. There are no other shoreline rocks with deep water beside them; my wharf, therefore, will remain inconvenient.)

Thus it was not until the aircraft was secured and the pilot had opened the door that the clients were revealed. To my surprise, they were all of retirement age; some were quite elderly. Most needed assistance to ease themselves down the narrow-runged plane ladder to the float and then step up onto the deck of the wharf; many had brought walking aids such as sticks—one even had a frame with him. (I learned later that the local stores did a wonderful business in broom handles.)

The ground around my cabins is hardly geared for those with walking disabilities and I was pretty apprehensive as to how the day would go. But I need not have worried. The vacationers were the most cheerful and enthusiastic crowd I could have wished for. Although some of them were hindered by it, very few let the terrible ground daunt them and we hobbled slowly around the place to see a few points of interest. The first tour did not arrive until mid-August but, because of the craziness of the season, there were still quite a lot of flowers in the nearby meadows and the visitors, many of them naturalists, were delighted. Most were from Victoria, which flower-starred city is host to an enormous range of blossoms both cultivated and wild; but many of my common old weeds were observed with wonder, for alpine varieties do not take kindly to that city's Mediterranean climate. It is nice to think they can't have everything. The fact that the meadows were still a tad wet, causing some of the tourists to step in bogholes and lose shoes, fazed them not a bit. I well remember one couple, where the husband was almost blind but otherwise fit, and the wife bent over with whatever ailed her, but she hung on to him for support, somewhat in the manner of the operators of a pantomime horse, and gave him the benefit of her eyes, and they went around the place in fine style.

I had been asked to supply refreshments—fortunately I had just enough mugs on the place to give everyone a drink at the same time.

I am not much of a cook and certainly no cake-maker, but I do bake tasty, heavy bread. Because of the small size of my stove-pipe oven, it had taken all the previous day to make the three batches I figured would be necessary. Whatever container will

fit the inadequate space in the oven is used—billy cans and roasting dishes mostly—but I have a small bread pan which I generally squeeze in somehow when visitors are due. It has quite a history for it was given to me twenty years ago in New Zealand by an eighty-year-old neighbour who claimed it was her mother's. This pan was a minor casualty during one of the bear break-ins. It sports a single imploded gash in the side where a tooth must have penetrated. The gash is faithfully modeled by the rising dough, thus every loaf of bread pops out complete with the bear's tooth mark indented into it.

I had one other bear artifact to show the visitors; providence had fortuitously laid it on my doorstep especially for the season.

The day after I arrived home in the spring, I took the short walk to the little meadow north of the cabin to see how many of the big winter drifts still remained and whether or not any of the early flowers were managing to bloom. Not more than three hundred yards from my house, at the exact spot in which I had pitched the tent while building the guest cabin, was evidence of a considerable drama. Ground vegetation, mostly crowberry and Labrador tea, had been raked up from an area as large as a good-sized living room and formed into what must have been a sizable mound before time and its agents had flattened it. From the remains of the heap protruded a dozen sharp, white slivers of bone and several sections of a chunky, much-chewed spine whose vertebrae were at least the size of those of the cows I cut up and preserved in jars during the winter. Grey, dog-like droppings full of bone chips were scattered throughout the area.

I am a great fan of such authors as P.D. James and Elizabeth

George, and here was a murder mystery, right on my doorstep, for me to solve all by myself.

The dog-like droppings were obviously those of wolves, but although they had apparently finished the carcass off, they would never have attempted to bury it. There are no cougars up this far, so the burial could only be the work of a bear. Bears think nothing is more delectable than a feed of flesh; the more rotten it is the better. They stake their claims on a carcass by covering it with debris (often soil, but none was available here) and their scent.

So the identity of the undertaker seemed clear enough, but the killer might not necessarily have been the same creature. The bear might well have come across the animal after it was already dead. It would very much help to sort the story out if I could identify the victim

The victim was large and so wolves as the killers at once came to mind. I have stumbled upon several wolf kills here, usually caribou, and, as the remains decompose, bear tracks often appear on the scene. Perhaps this had happened and a bear had come along and simply seized the carcass. But something about the evidence did not quite support this scenario. The vertebrae, which were the only recognizeable bits of anatomy except for a small section of a shoulder blade, seemed very large and thick for a caribou—perhaps the victim, therefore, was a moose. If that was so, however, moose vertebrae had to be far chunkier than those of a cow. There were clumps of hair among the dead sticks of the burial pile, hair which was sandy, an appropriate enough colour for a member of the deer family, but of the wrong texture. Instead of being straight, thick and hollow with a paintbrush-bristle quality, it was fine and soft and very slightly crinkly. There is only one animal that has hair like that, and my mind was already heading towards the inevitable conclusion, when I found the skull.

It was separate from the rest of the pile and half-hidden behind some bushes. It had been almost completely fleshed but amazingly, in view of the splintered remains of the rest of the carcass, there was not so much as a tooth mark on it. The victim, like the burier, was a bear.

Mysteriouser and mysteriouser! How did the victim die? Wolves would be unlikely to kill a bear unless it was very sick or old. The teeth of the skull were fairly worn so that might have been the case. But it seemed far more likely that the second bear had killed it. They do fight sometimes—grizzlies will slaughter black bears and males will kill and eat cubs as well as the cub's mother. My Atnarko landlords heard two grizzlies roaring and crashing close to their cabin for most of one night and, in the morning, found the carcass of a partially eaten sow. It was assumed she had been trying to defend her cubs although there was no sign of any young—perhaps they had been eaten as well. Maybe some of the splintered and broken vegetation around my old campsite was more than just an attempt to procure burial material; perhaps it was the result of such a battle.

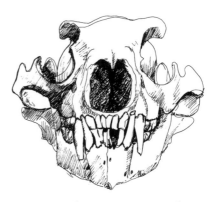

The executioner, however, could just as easily have been human. It might have been a legal hunter or it could have been a poacher. By keeping among gullies and valleys it is easy for a small aircraft to dodge surveillance in this country. If a human was involved, it would undoubtedly have been someone with an aircraft—no modern hunter would dream of walking so far from a road—and I would be less than pleased to think that someone flew over my meadow, saw the bear, landed at my wharf and bumped the animal off on my doorstep.

Unfortunately, the answer to the question remains sheer speculation. Whatever happened it must have been between the time I went out the previous October and before the snow flew, which means it was probably not very long after I had left. I came back in January and was here for three months, but the signs of the drama had been hidden beneath the snow.

The skull was pretty ripe but I was hardly going to let such a small inconvenience bother me. Here was a trophy of note indeed. But I would have to clean it up.

Burying bones to let soil creatures work on them, even if the right species of animals lived among these rocks, is not a very efficient way to clean carcasses in this dry, cool climate. Besides, the dogs or another bear would be only too delighted to dig up and make off with such a highly flavoursome tidbit. So I boiled the skull in an old bucket (with door and all windows of the cabin wide open) and scraped it and boiled it and scraped it again and eventually tied it to the roof ladder to let the sun, weather and chickadees finish the job through the summer. I have a large collection of rocks, wood, shells and other natural forms, products of years of travel in a multitude of wilderness areas, but this skull is special. Within the convoluted chambers of the bones and the ivory spears of the teeth hang the spirits of Nuk Tessli: the *kami,* the wildness, the soul. I can see myself now, in the old people's home, with the skull on my bedside table, the one final treasure I will take with me to the end.

Could the victim possibly be Gold Tip? Had he finally met his comeuppance by a hand (or paw) other than mine? The fur in the burial pile was much lighter than I remembered his coat to be, but that might have been the result of bleaching as it lay out in the weather. There seemed to be no bears in the meadow during the spring, for the dogs did not bark all season. But with the cold, late year, so much of nature was out of sync that my usual ursine spring neighbours, whoever they might be, could simply have been feeding elsewhere. It is unfortunate that I don't know for certain, for I cannot afford to dispense with the trap: however, that ugly contraption does have a use over and above its designated purpose. With the possible exception of the dogs, now that the bus tours have come, it must be the most photographed object on the place.


Death, one way and another, was quite a feature of the west Chilcotin that year. There were several human casualties and they all made the news for the causes of death were unusual enough to excite the media. Three climbers were killed on Mt. Monarch by an avalanche (very close to the moraines I wanted to botanize) and the survivors took four days to walk out and reach help; a man on horseback was attacked by a black bear in Tatlyoko about fifty miles south of my cabin—the horse bolted and dumped the man, and the bear killed and ate part of him. And a young pilot misjudged the turbulent southwest winds over Knot Lake and crashed and drowned—it is always the young ones that go; flying school, I am afraid, does not seem to teach their pupils much about mountain winds.

The number of wilderness fatalities was certainly higher than usual that year but, overall, injury or death in the wilderness is of no greater or lesser consequence than that which occurs in other places. City people like to hear about wilderness tragedies, though—they are more colourful than freeway pile-ups and they reassure city dwellers of the wildness they all still need at the fringes of their existence, no matter how they rationalize its extinction, or how sedentary they prefer their own lives to be. We each take our chances with our environments, and if danger from bears and planes and avalanches loom closer to me than to the average city-dweller, I am not the one who locks my doors, and I am far less likely to be run over by a bus.

I did not know any of the human victims in the area so I could not be affected by them other than to feel a detached compassion. But there was a death at the end of that summer with which I was directly involved. It wasn't a human death, it was one of my dogs'— what was worse, I had to be the one who initiated it.

Sport was reaching the end of his useful life. Unlike Lonesome, he was not a charismatic animal. His temperament was fine for he was good natured and gentle, but for some years he had suffered severe allergies, due to the chemicals in commercial dog food, which gave him the most terrible skin infections and an aroma which turned even the staunchest dog-lover away. With me at home he was not too much of a problem for he lived outside and, apart from a continuous need to scratch, he ate well and still seemed to be enjoying life. He was also, for all of his complaining, an excellent packdog. I tried expensive food, medicated baths and ear douches to alleviate the allergy problems, but in the end only a steady diet of a cortisone derivative kept him on an even keel. This was all very expensive—the drug was cheap enough, just a few bucks—but the vets refused to give it to me until they had examined the dog themselves and as I knew perfectly well what was wrong with him and how to deal with it, the necessity of driving Sport to Williams Lake and the $80 I was charged each time was hard to swallow.

For a friend to keep him on would be expensive; he could not be tolerated inside because of his allergies; outside, if he was tied up he whined and if he was loose he headed straight for the nearest garbage can. He also suffered from chronic motion sickness so it was no fun to take him anywhere. In the fall of that year, *Diary of a Wilderness*

*Dweller* was to be launched and an extensive book-promotion tour was woven into the craft-fair circuit, all of which would involve a great deal of driving. Taya would be able to come along, in fact I knew she would be an asset for she would be the star of my slide shows. But for Sport the journey would be miserable.

It is a city fallacy to ascribe simplicity to wilderness living. The townsman attributes his tensions to the multitude of urban-oriented schemes with which he has entangled his life, and consoles himself that, without his sacrifices, civilization would die. He assumes the growing of food and the daily acquaintance of nature to be an uncomplicated business, for when he comes to the wilderness, it is on vacation, where, if he sees nothing but peace and serenity, it is because his host has done all the groundwork to make it that way.

To me, it is city life that is simple. There, all the unpleasant things are taken care of for you. There is no drudgery—water, power and communication are available at the push of a button; smelly things like sewage and garbage magically disappear; meat is tidily packaged away from the blood, viscera and the last, gurgling breath; children are baby-sat and educated (after a fashion) by the school system; funeral directors deal with the deceased; and vets dispose of unwanted animals.

The trip from Nuk Tessli to the nearest vet requires a day and a half's walk plus five hours in a car. It would certainly have been easier for me to shelve the responsibility of dealing with Sport and let someone else do it, but for the dog, it seemed kinder to do the deed myself. Despite my attempt with Gold Tip on the porch, I had never actually killed an animal larger than a rabbit.

The thought of Sport's demise hung over me like a shadow. I considered waiting for a friend who was due to arrive, a man who hunts and is used to shooting deer for food. Surely killing a dog he did not own would not be as traumatic for him as it would be for me? But it is not the sort of thing you can ask a friend to do. I waited until no one else was around, chained Taya to the cabin, and took Sport far into the bush where bears that found the carcass would not become a danger. I gave the dog a pat and a favourite treat; while he was deliriously wolfing it down, I shot him.

# chapter 20

# the way of the wilderness dweller

*Off the trail is another name for The Way. And sauntering off
the trail is the practice of the wild. You must first be on the path
before you can turn and walk into the wild.*

Gary Snyder, *The Practice of The Wild*

I was enormously surprised the first time someone demanded a reason for my decision to live in the bush. Isn't it obvious? I thought.
Doesn't everyone rave about the beauties of the wilderness? The challenge, the satisfaction, the *rightness* of living close to nature? Why do
I need to explain this to people? And yet the same question is asked
every time I am interviewed. If the answer is so obvious, why do
people continue to ask it? And why do I have such difficulty in making a reply? I cite the usual aphorisms: a rural upbringing; craftsman
parents from whom I learned a lot of the necessary skills without
being aware of it; being, for whatever reason, a loner; a nature-lover;
no dependents; clean air; a greater control over one's way of life. But
my sibling, who surely had much the same influences in his child-
hood as myself, lives happily in the same house and village in England
in which we grew up, and is now ensconced in the kind of rural sub-
urbia that is so popular these days.

It was a man called Gary Snyder who gave me an insight into my own basic philosophy. I am suspicious of what I perceive to be fashionable religions, so was somewhat reluctant to read a book by the California Zen Buddhist that was leant to me by a friend. But the friend was insistent that "I would be bound to like it" and the very fact of having my friend's personal thoughts entrusted to me surely denoted a measure of respect towards him, if not for the author. So, upon seeing the book one day and realizing I should have returned it long ago, I opened its pages.

The book was Gary Snyder's *Practice of the Wild*. I thought some of Snyder's initial dissertations not very relevant to my situation, but eventually found myself drawn into the book to such a degree I even committed some of the writer's words to a notebook I keep for favourite quotations.

Not that I felt Snyder was saying anything new. His book deals primarily with our relationship to the living ecosystem of our planet. Like myself, he believes that humans are just another cog in the wheel of the great and complicated machine that comprises our environment. If we keep to the grooves for which we are designed and don't try and replace other bits of the machinery, the gears will mesh smoothly; if we jump out of our tracks, something has got to give.

We have heard a multitude of similar analogies over the last twenty or thirty years. The Gaia Movement and other environmental groups have come into being. But I had a respect for the physiological purpose of all living creatures long before I ever heard of the word "environmentalist." I understood that all species are inter-related long before the Gaia Movement ever became celebrated. I have always known these things. I cannot remember not knowing them. And it was not because Gary Snyder elaborated upon this theme that I became enlightened, but because of the *way* he expounded it. He wrote as if his audience did *not* know these things. The world, it would appear, has other theories about its placement within the cosmos.

This revelation hit me like a ton of bricks. But at once, several things fell into place. Take the words, for instance, of a syndicated columnist published in the Bella Coola paper a few years ago. The writer was commenting on the furor as to whether or not the Stein Valley should be logged. He wrote that keeping such a huge area of land intact was nonsense; he had taken his family to a picnic ground at the edge of his city over the weekend and everyone had lots of fun—what was the point in preserving vast areas that very few people could get into?

He, an apparently intelligent human being, really believed that a scattering of picnic grounds were all that the world required to stay healthy.

From where do such people get their ideas? Do they not eat, grow, breathe, bleed, procreate, defecate, expire and eventually decompose (despite chemical attempts to prevent them) like every other living organism? Do they really consider themselves separate entities from nature?

If they are not part of nature, what are they?


The realization that one's whole *raison d'être*—which was so entrenched that it had never been questioned let alone come to the surface, is not shared by the world at large—is somewhat disturbing. Despite living a two- to four-day hike from the closest community I had not thought I was so very different from everyone else; I need (and have) food, shelter, comfort, human contact, mental stimulation, entertainment and toilet paper.

And yet I have been called eccentric, and that amazed me. It can only be because my life was not formulated by the peculiar conditioning inherent in the microcosm of a North American city. Are not the overloaded materialism, stink, noise, stress and remoteness from reality eccentricities? Why on earth should I embrace such meaninglessness in order to conform with a deluded and unthinking populace?

Interestingly enough, many city dwellers might claim to despise these same aspects of their lives. But they obviously don't dislike them enough to want to do anything about them. And when people continue to choose a lifestyle they claim to abhor, especially when the majority have the brains, health and money to change it, something is out of whack.

If my philosophy is so different from that of the majority, from where do I get it? I don't ever remember being told all this stuff, although something must have planted the seed at some stage. My brother lives in what most people these days would refer to as the country. But there is a constant stream of traffic past his door and, whereas he is very competent and knowledgeable about many things, he probably wouldn't know a carrot from a daffodil if it was growing in the garden (he might recognize them on his plate) or a thrush from a sparrow. And if he, a man with influence, knows so little about the planet's vast and complicated workings, how can he possibly make informed decisions about them?

When I initiated my wilderness venture it never occurred to me to qualify my reasons either to myself or to anyone else. Here was an opportunity I thought I could handle, there was nothing else that I wanted to do *more*, and I took it. While it might have been pleasurably adventurous, the idea did not seem at all extraordinary. Convention, or lack of it, or a need to explain myself, never entered my mind.

But I now see it all stems from that innermost philosophy that was always present but had remained undefined; the rightness of having an awareness of and living close to the natural world. To me this relationship with the planet is not merely a period of play to be indulged in during the summer, or even for a year or two as some people do. It is a conviction so forceful that I would simply be unable to live in any other way.

# chapter 21

## *nature immersion*

*I thought of the long ages of the past, during which the successive generations of this little creature had run their course ... amid these dark and gloomy woods with no intelligent eye to gaze upon their loveliness; to all appearances such a wanton waste of beauty ... It seems sad that ... such exquisite creatures should live out their lives and exhibit their charms only in these wild, inhospitable regions. (But) should civilized man ever reach these distant lands and bring moral, intellectual, and physical light into the recesses of these virgin forests, we may be sure he will so disturb the nicely balanced relations of organic and inorganic nature as to cause the disappearance, and finally the extinction, of these very beings whose wonderful structure and beauty he alone is fitted to appreciate and enjoy. This consideration must surely tell us that all living things were not made for man.*

Alfred Russel Wallace, *The Malay Archipelago (1869)*

Formal education is, and always has been, the product of a city mind. All through history, groups of people have separated themselves from the rest of society, removed themselves from the mechanics of producing their food and shelter, and demanded that others supply these basic necessities of life. Thus, the city dweller was born. By excluding toil and drudgery from his existence, he discovered leisure. His time and energy could therefore be spent upon pursuits other than feeding and clothing himself; among these was the invention of codes to create records.

A city dweller and a country dweller have differing points of view about many things. The country dweller knows this for a lot of the city-man's dogma fail to apply to him; the townsman, however, has little notion that his own theories might not be universally acceptable. He has been brainwashed through countless generations into thinking that his solutions to life are absolute. The whole world is poorer for his ignorance.

When the incipient townsman looked out upon the gardens and fields that surrounded his palaces, all that he could see were weariness, drudgery and grime. The peasant, because he had neither the energy, nor in many cases the permission, to learn the symbols the townsman had devised, was declared stupid. Whatever knowledge the peasant might have possessed was effaced by his supposed inferiority; it was consequently never valued and therefore, more important, never written down. And because it had no place in the city-man's records, it soon ceased, in the city mind, to exist.

The peasant, unfortunately, would contribute to this situation. Firstly, the knowledge that he had accumulated would be largely unrealised even by himself. On the one hand, he would have absorbed a wealth of information during his daily life in the same way that a child learns a language, without having much more idea than the townsman that he knew a great deal of value; on the other, he would have been brainwashed into the belief of his own inferiority. If the peasant should be so fortunate as to shrug off his lowly status, he would, in turn, despise his one-time contemporaries and the labour they represented. Even if he had been aware of any knowledge that he possessed, he would be loath to admit it in case it might point to the baseness of his origins. Thus was information irretrievably lost. Today, we can transplant hearts, but we no longer know how the Incas cut massive blocks of stone with absolute precision but without what we recognize as tools.

Not too long ago, in central British Columbia, a group of native Indians protested a proposed golf course and luxury vacation development on what they claimed was land of traditional native significance. Some of the protesters were militant; they dressed themselves in combat fatigues and armed themselves with rifles. Shots were fired.

The authorities responded by the method they used to smoke out armed malefactors in a city. They erected a blockade. I happened to be outside while this was going on, and I caught a TV news broadcast giving an update. The announcer was expounding: "City tactics are simply not going to work. They cannot cut off the water because the natives are camping by a lake. They cannot cut off sewage because they simply shit in the bush." (She didn't word it *quite* like that.) "They cannot cut off electricity because there isn't any. Food is supplied by people coming in over the hills on horseback and on foot and what they can catch in the wild."

I was stunned. Not because of what the announcer was saying, but because of her incredulous manner. She was amazed! It was a revelation!

She was astounded at the natives' perspicacity: I was dumfounded at the city-man's ignorance. The authorities should not have needed to learn that city tactics would not work. Any country dweller would have understood the logistics of the situation at once. Even more astounding, the great revelation was announced *three weeks* after the blockade had been started. It had taken that long for the authorities to figure it out.

Literature often cites that the Canadian character, culture, art or whatever, is derived from our country's wildness. That, I am afraid, stopped with Catherine Parr Traill. In the above example, as in many others, it was not the city dweller's inability to think in a rural way that was so disturbing, but the fact that he took so long to understand that his approach was irrelevant.

And people with this kind of background claim to be able to make competent decisions about our environment.

The city-man's disregard of how the world really works leads to a curious paradox. The city dweller has had to admit that the peasant possesses skills that the former can no longer emulate. But, reasons the city dweller, these skills cannot be the result of education. Education is tangible; it is a finite entity measured by our own perfectly crafted symbols. We invented it; it has to be right. The country dweller, in his ability to achieve something outside these parameters, must therefore have something non-tangible in his makeup. Non-tangible means supernatural: the peasant has become a mystic.

And yet all he has is knowledge that anyone can learn.

Presented with the enormous complexities of a viable ecosystem, the average townsman will balk at his inadequacy to assimilate it. And an adult conditioned to city-speak would indeed have a mammoth task ahead of him. It would be like trying to assimilate a foreign language, only worse. For there are no six-session crash courses in environmental consciousness to be had.

It has got to start with the children, otherwise nature becomes, to them, either a Hollywoodized anthropomorphism or just as mysterious as the workings of my computer are to me. French immersion schools are considered all-important in Canadian society, but what about nature immersion schools? A second language, while it is not to be decried, is no more than a means to expand communications between a small selection of our particular species of animal, all of whom constitute only a fraction of our world's organisms.

Oh, environmental studies are taught in city classrooms, but they are taught as separate subjects, like basketball or geography; something that you play with for thirty minutes a week and then shelve as being irrelevant to the real scheme of things. The programs are written by city dwellers, the teachers are city dwellers themselves, with the same inherent cultural influences; environmental concepts thus remain a package apart. It is cool to save the whales and camp out with tribal elders who are blocking a logging road. But a life without a stereo, an air-conditioned car, the latest hi-tech skis or a career in economics? What's that got to do with grizzly bears?

The earth is often referred to as a global village. A global city is a much more accurate analogy. City dwellers' myths, standards and prejudices are now perpetuated at an unprecedented scale. We are no longer nibbling at isolated environments, which cannot be affected much more than a days' walk beyond the nearest centre of population, but at the whole world at once.

People who question leaving the city while their kids are still in school, worried that they might "miss out on something" should think again. To teach a child that he belongs in an interdependent ecosystem that deserves respect is surely the greatest, almost the only, inheritance that he or she needs.

# chapter 22

# *the shell game*

*And now, having touched upon almost every subject likely to prove useful to the emigrant's wife or daughter, in her Canadian home, I will take my leave, with the sincere hope that some among my readers may derive profit and assistance from the pages, which, with much toil and pains, I have written for their instruction ...*

*If I have sometimes stepped aside to address the men, on matters that were connected with their department ... such hints I hope may well be taken ... for the ultimate benefit and comfort of all.*

Catherine Parr Traill, *The Canadian Settler's Guide*

Nuk Tessli's tenth year marks the advent of a logging plan that made a bid for a thick peppering of cutblocks over a vast tract of land north of Nimpo Lake (much of which is traditional first nations food-gathering territory) as well as large sections of the Charlotte Alplands. Most of this would be cut in a single season; a good proportion would be beetle-kill blocks and therefore extra to the Annual Allowable Cut, and it would all come under the aegis of the small business program. By the year 2002, if this proposal was to go through, trees would be logged to within three miles of my cabins.

It is possible that the Charlotte Alplands Committee will be able to influence a few restrictions regarding some of the ecological impact. In a sensitive area "only" sixty percent of the blocks can be clearcut, and some concessions would be made, in principle at any rate, to riparian strips along the main waterways.

The slated cutblocks are in the slightly better pockets of timber in the area, mostly spruce, where a big tree is sixty feet tall and fifteen inches thick at the butt, all on north- and east-facing slopes where the snow lies late and the ground remains damp well into the summer. During my eight years as a tree-planter, mostly at higher elevations, I often plodded upward, on a baking hot, naked slope, slotting trees in the ground every three or four paces, knowing that the only relief to the mind-numbing heat would be at the top. There, shade from the unlogged forest would cut thirty degrees off the temperature and there might well be the exquisite reward of a revitalising patch of snow. Despite the baked desert of the open block, this blessed strip of shadow might harbour ground that was still frozen. At higher elevations, the climate difference between shaded and open ground is extreme. Nobody seems to have bothered to feed that kind of information into the computers yet.

Logging such blocks cannot fail to have an enormous effect on the timing and volume of runoff in the spring. As the area dubbed the Charlotte Alplands constitutes almost the greater part of the watershed for the principal branch of the third-largest salmon spawning river in British Columbia, it is hard to see how fish breeding cycles could not be affected. And the already precarious defenses of the flood plain that comprises much of the inhabited land in the Bella Coola Valley may well be unable to cope. Industrial scientists will claim they have calculated all contingencies and no harm will ensue, but such claims have never yet been proven right. And I wonder if anyone cares about this? By the time ecological disasters happen, profits have been made and the problem is someone else's. Once a tree is cut down, or a chunk of land has slid into a river, one cannot push the "undo" button, as one can on a computer, and make the image right again.

Analyses to determine the economic potential of country like this is not done in the field. People simply sit at computers and draw on information from previous reports. The only actual data about the wildlife that seems to be extant for this area is an old logging survey done more than thirty years ago. This looked at commercial trees only and ignored other plants and all animals. The word "biodiversity" crops up in the report, but in the logging industry's typically ambiguous fashion, this refers only to the disparity of age in a stand of trees and has nothing to do with non-commercial species. These out of date and grossly misleading figures still form the only species records used for land-use decisions. More recently both a lake survey and a general species survey have been completed: how this data will be used remains to be seen.

Exactly how logging the Charlotte Alplands will affect Nuk Tessli is a matter for speculation. It could well make my life more convenient—I might be able to travel in and out for mail in a single day. It may make my business more lucrative; for the number of tourists would surely increase. Perhaps I will be entertaining ATV-ers and snowmachiners as well as hikers and naturalists. And my new-found wealth would probably just pay for the increased taxes, rents and insurance premiums, and the array of locks on my doors.

The visitors who drove up the logging roads and walked the remaining few miles to my place would still revel in the landscape that is left. Snow would still fall, the sunrise would still illuminate the mountains, and the Coast Range would spread in wave upon wave of awesome pinnacle and ice. As momentoes of their brief, euphoric communication with the untouched wild, the visitors would place cairns, dig fire pits, wear vehicular tracks and strew garbage. And that priceless and mysterious force, product of billions of years of chance and evolution, that mystical and uncreatable spark that is an untouched ecosystem, would start to erode.

Hold in your hand a whelk shell washed up on the beach and marvel at the intricacies of creation. Beyond its erotic whorls and convolutions is a subtler fascination, for it speaks of romance and sea-change and mysteries only partially understood. But the shell is just that: beautiful, awe-inspiring and empty. Life created it, but the life force is no longer within it. No machinations known to man can ever put it back.

The shell has no other destiny than disintegration.

Chris Czajkowski grew up on the edge of a village in the north of England. Natural history always fascinated her, and she trained in agriculture, specifically the dairy industry. Once qualified, she travelled to Uganda where she taught at a farm school for a year. Chris then travelled widely through Asia, before arriving in New Zealand. There she worked primarily on commercial dairy farms and sheep stations and spent her spare time exploring the beautiful scenery and discovering the flora and fauna of the region. It was in New Zealand that she first began to sell her watercolour paintings of the scenery and wildflowers.

After travelling through the South Pacific and South America, Chris emigrated to Canada. Attracted by the mountains of British Columbia, she eventually came to roost in an area of the Coast Range near Bella Coola, 300 miles north of Vancouver. She built a log house twenty-seven miles from the road and accessible only by foot and canoe. Through her letters to Peter Gzowski in the 1980s, she became a regular contributor to CBC Radio's "Morningside" program. Her adventures during that time became the basis for her second book, *Cabin at Singing River* (Camden House, 1991).

*Diary of a Wilderness Dweller* (Orca Book Publishers, 1996) is the story of her time spent building a second cabin, this time a mere twenty-mile walk from the nearest road. This cabin is located on a high altitude, fly-in lake, from which she guides artists and naturalists on backpacking trips amidst the magnificent mountains that surround her. Living at such an altitude and so far from a road gives Chris a unique opportunity to study the wildlife in an area that has had so little documentation that much of it remains unnamed.

Chris travels throughout the Pacific Northwest giving slide shows to local botanical and alpine garden clubs, book stores and libraries. To arrange for a visit from Chris please contact Orca Book Publishers or the author directly at the address below.

The Nuk Tessli Alpine Experience offers two self-contained wilderness cabins for rent (you fly to the door), and/or guided day hikes or overnight backpacking trips. There are no fixed routes or schedules, activities are geared to the abilities and interests of the individuals. For more information write to: Chris Czajkowski, Nuk Tessli Alpine Experience, Nimpo Lake, BC V0L 1R0, or phone Avnorth Aviation, 250-742-3285.